We All Have Choices

You can smile, even through your tears, no matter which road you end up taking those steps.

Laurie Delk

1st Edition

Introduction 3
Getting Started 7

Happiness 12
We have the choice to be happy...12

Eating 32
We have the choice as to what we put in our mouth 32

Fitness 45
We have the choice to get on that treadmill 45

Health 56
We have the choice to listen to our body's needs..............56

Business 69
We have the choice to do activities to help our business .69

Talking 82
We have the choice to do think before we speak 82

Relationships - Personal 95
We have the choice to build our personal relationships..95

Relationships - Business 105
We have the choice to build our business relationships.105

Thinking 111
We have the choice to think positively or negatively, prosperously or poorly..111

Jesus 120
We have the choice to follow, accept Jesus 120

Choosing You 125
Today is not an end; it is a beginning. Start today! 125

Introduction

We all go through many "roller coasters" in life. God kept convicting me to write a book after I lost Bryan, my husband of 20 years, and father of my children in a tragic car wreck February 2, 2013. I kept thinking and arguing with God, "What am I going to write about? What could I possibly teach people?"

So many people I looked up to, in my business and my personal life, that I thought were much more qualified than me. But, anyone who knows, when God convicts you on something, you will "not win" if you choose to not do it, or try not to! :)

I first thought of smiling, Bryan used to always say, "I want to see you smile." I remember thinking one day, while I was crying, him looking down from Heaven saying this exact thing to me. The thought in my head, "He would not want me to be like this, and I am not being a good example to my children, nor others around me that might possibly look up to me."

A lightbulb, a God moment — if you will — "You can smile, even through your tears". I thought that was going to be the title of my book. So i started writing, and thinking about chapters, etc...

Through much procrastination, and still yet arguing with God that there are many books out there and many others way more capable than me, and over the next couple years, this word, this concept, kept popping into my head, "choices."

We all have a choice to what we do in life, what we think, what we put in our mouths, what we say to ourself and to others, how we react — so many choices — We All Have Choices, and we can choose wisely or poorly, and either way we will suffer or enjoy the consequences of those choices.

Through the next few years of attempting to start writing this book, and making "choices" to put it off, saying to myself, I am too busy, I will start later, and so many more excuses. If we want excuses, we can find them in anything and anywhere.

In some ways, excuses can be challenges to God.

After losing my husband, I didn't think I would have to deal with loss for a long time. Yet, only 6 months after losing Bryan, I lost our family dog of 13 years. He was our sweet Boxer named Bullet. Then I lost my Grandfather, (my dad's dad) who I grew up staying at their house many weekends when I was little. March 2014 comes along, and we lost Bryan's father. He lived in our garage apartment, and we had cared for him for 15 years. My 28-year-old daughter was diagnosed with Non-Hodgkins Lymphoma Cancer in June of 2015, and then in November 2015, my mother (who was also one of my best friends in life) was diagnosed with Ovarian cancer. My daughter chose chemo plus natural things and was thankfully announced cancer free in December that year. My mother, unfortunately, we lost her in March 2016, three weeks before my parents 50th anniversary, and huge surprise party my sisters and I had planned for them. Later in 2016, October, we lost my Bryan's Grandaddy (where my kids played on his farm and worked too, many days growing up). And most recently, his Granny Grace in July 2017.

Yes, the past few years have been some of the craziest twist and turns life's roller coaster has to offer. Also the different shoes I have been given to walk through life in, and the choices of how we walk in those shoes, can make all the difference in the world.

Each twist and turn and upside down moment is the opportunity to find an excuse or to find a reason. Excuses are made by those who are lazy or comfortable where they are. When we seek a true change, a true change in our mindset and in our lives, we find a reason to do it.

That reason is our motivation.

Instead of using all of the loss my family and I have experienced to not do something, I am seeing it as a way to impact others, to impact myself, to inspire. My choice in moving forward, in a thank you to Bryan, my Grandfather, Bryan's Grandaddy, my daughter, and my mother, as well as others, and a thank you for you also, choosing to believe in me, and making the choice to hear and read my story.

Your choice is an inspiration. It is one that will inspire others. It is a choice of confidence ~ in yourself, taking the time for you, and confidence in what this book/story can offer to you.

Getting Started

What does "getting started mean?" Simply get started. Make the right choices in your life today, in every aspect of your life. It is a choice. Choose to make choices that will benefit you, your children, your family or others around you.

What is a choice? What does choice mean? Choice is simply finding an opportunity and deciding on an option because you have picked a preference what you desire to do or not to do next. And, what you must always remember, you deciding to not take action is still a choice. No one makes you do anything. You always have choice in every situation. Every situation! It is called "Free Will" God gave us that choice, and instilled it into us when we were created. He gives us guidelines of His rulebook in the Bible, and we can learn it, teach it, read it, etc. But we have the choice to follow it or what we do with it in every aspect of our lives.

Think before you make any decision, say a word, take an action, if it is the right choice for you. Some people say pray about it, some people say ask yourself, or ask your higher or inner self, some people say ask your holy spirit. It doesn't matter what you believe, in the end, God made our Universe, and all that is within it. So use what you choose, there is that choice again we all have, and make the choices every day to guide you best, to your best for your life.

Every day, wth every decision that you make, or every time before you speak, think for a minute, "Is this the right choice for me to say or do, before saying or doing it?"

Why is it so important to think about every decision you make? Does it seem you won't have any time to make decisions if you are always thinking about them?

By taking the time to think, we are slowing down our actions, our reactions. We are being congruent to who we say we are in this world. We are giving our heart and our mind a chance to process what is about to happen, the consequences (good or bad) of our choices.

If we know what to expect, if we know how our choices will affect us and those around us, we can see the good or not so good in our choices. This allows more time in our lives because we aren't reacting to negative situations caused by us.

You have the freedom, the power, and the ability to choose what to do. The choices you will make (from this moment on) will show to you and everyone around you how you choose to live your life.

It sounds super easy, right? But it can be the hardest thing to do. The decision to make a choice and then to live with it, as that is what creates **your** life.

Sometimes, we even make choices without even noticing or paying attention. We just do like we are robots without the ability to make a conscious choice. Like choosing a protein bar over salmon and asparagus at a meal. Choosing to take or ignore a call. Choosing to write (or not to write) in our gratitude journal before bed. Choosing which job to take. Choosing which friends to go out with this weekend. Choosing to stay in or end a relationship. Choosing to respond to that call or text.

How you feel can play a part in the choices you make, if you allow it. When you are in a negative, complaining, bitter mood, your choices more than likely, will not be as wise as when you are in a positive, grateful, happy mood.

Life is full of choices. And, every choice you make is going to have consequences. It can either make you a stronger and better person or it can ruin you and make you feel more inferior leaving you trusting others less. Which sounds like the better choice? Of course, most of us, I would think all of us, would want the first, to feel stronger, better, more confident. With that, we have choices in our life we can make, to help us and guide us in that direction, every single day, every single moment.

Trust yourself. Trust your instincts. Focus on the decisions you have to make and think about them in your mind and in your heart. Breathe in deep through your nose, then "Pah" out deep through your mouth. Continue deep relaxing breaths while you focus on your choice to make. Feel it in your gut and in your emotions. When it is wrong for you, you will tend to feel tense and uneasy. If it is right for you, you will tend to feel happy, relaxed and more sure of yourself. Feel these feelings; notice them in your own body when you feel them. Learn to be in tune with your own feelings, your own inner spirit, that is leading and guiding you to see more of yourself.

Recognize, you always have a choice. Take a step back, breathe, and think about the consequences of your actions. Take it even further by processing if they are in your best interest. Be aware. Be mindful. Life can be both easy and hard. Sometimes it knocks you down or brings you to your knees. But, in everything, there is always something for which to be grateful — even if it is nothing more than that pretty blue vase on the wall. See it, feel it, be grateful and feel the gratitude for it and its beauty.

When you make the choice to focus on the things in which you can be grateful and thankful for, you will automatically attract more things and events in your life to be more grateful and thankful for. You can call it karma, what comes around goes around, the universe, God, etc., whatever you want …

It is still truth, and God created our universe. God tells us to control our thoughts and what to think in the Bible. He never says to dwell on unhappy or sad things or things that make us angry or mad. Those are all emotions and many times they will come up, and we will have full just cause for thinking them … But, the thing is we must not "stay there" in those thoughts, we must find the grateful and thankful thing within whatever that is, and focus on that.

When I first heard of Bryan's wreck, all that positivity went right out the window. I was crushed. I cried so much. I was mad and angry. I even played the "what if" games in my mind. In situations, we will tend to do that sometimes and have every justification for doing so. I had so many great friends reach out to me in person, via text, calls, and even cards to love and comfort me in my time of need. I remember one specific card a great friend sent to me, with a poem in it called "He is gone." It basically reminded me to think and dwell on the twenty wonderful years God gave us to be together and have the kind of love that we had, rather than focus on the next twenty years that we were not going to have together.

"Finally, brethren, whatsoever things are true, whatsoever things are honest, whatsoever things are just, whatsoever things are pure, whatsoever things are lovely, whatsoever things are of good report; if there be any virtue, and if there be any praise, think on these things."

Philippians 4:8

Never choose to live as you are stone cold. Get started today. One thing to bring warmth to you heart. One truth to get your heart to make it through one more day. Sometimes all you need is one day to turn it all around. Happiness is right around the corner (or the next page)!

Chapter Number 1
Happiness
We have the choice to be happy

People will continue to do what they have always done until the hurt is so much that they cannot continue. Until there is no other choice, but to change. Change is a choice. Love is a choice. Happiness is a choice. That choice is a process. Life is a process. Enjoy it and be grateful in the process.

Choice is what separates human beings from all other mammals in the world ... all other animals in the world ... all other parts of nature. They simply do what they have been designed to do.

We have the opportunity to choose. A true gift from God. And, choice, means everything.

"These things I have spoken unto you, that in me ye might have peace. In the world ye shall have tribulation: but be of good cheer; I have overcome the world."
John 16:33

God tells us that we are going to "go thru things" — Even from an early age. No where in the "Book of Life" do we get the inclination that life is all good. Not even in song. But, maybe through a song, we can learn, "Don't Worry, Be Happy."

Even in song, we learn there are choices. We have to choose not to worry. We have to choose to be happy now.

We all do, and we all will go through the trials life that life can, does and will offer to us. The key thing is how you (how we) react to those things. In everything, you can find something to be grateful and thankful. Everything! Choose to be happy right now.

There is a song by the band Kutless and the words sing, "You are good, good, oh …." Your beliefs is your belief. It holds true for you. My belief is that He is good, good, oh …./ And, with that there can be only JOY. Real Happiness. Even I noted dark — alone — when we feel morning will never break, those night on insomnia, we can remember and focus on the real happiness we can and must choose to have. It is a fierce joy that washes over you when you let it.

I remember the end of 2008, I was so excited, I was pregnant with baby number 5!

Since I was in my late 30's, we chose to "wait to announce" as they say. I had just hit 5 month mark, as I began designing and planning our Christmas cards. We thought we were out of the "danger zone." There in our Christmas cards to several thousand people, we announced our exciting news! It was a thrilling and happy moment for our friends and family.

Then, as New Year's quickly approached, I decided it was time to set my resolution for 2009. My New Year's resolution for 2009 was to start a "Gratitude Journal."

When we decide we want something, God will show us just how to earn it! When I bought that beautiful, bold hot pink, sparkly journal, the adventure was set to begin. I was eager to start writing January 1st. (Anyone who knows me or gets to know me, understands what pink and sparkly means in my life!)

I awoke at 7 a.m. New Year's Day, went to the restroom, and saw blood. The tears welling up; I started crying. I just knew, right then. I called my midwife; then, I yelled for Bryan. Since he was a protector by nature, he took me to the hospital immediately.

It's in those moments of heartaches, we learn how easily the world chooses to judge us. As I waited, I overheard someone say "That's what she gets." (While some of the nurses, doctors and other people that took care of me, I know loved me and tried to help me the best that they could at that time, some of them also chose to believe a story made up in their minds by implying I was out partying the night before. Although, little did they know, I was at a church activity the night before, and didn't drink or smoke, ever.)

Of course with all my other emotions running wild, you can imagine that comment really hurt. The doctors and nurses did what they had to do, and sent me home.

When I arrived home, I saw my Gratitude journal on my bed. My heart hurt, and I thought, "Really? What am I supposed to write about and be thankful for, especially today?" Then, like a bolt of lightning sparkling in the reflection of my eyes, God convicted my heart. Yes, He reminded me - I had 4 other beautiful and totally healthy children for whom I should, and in fact, must, be thankful for.

It was a choice to see the happiness, to understand the joy, to react in a way that God desires us to — to seek Him and to allow Him to show us joy and gratitude in our lives.

> *"I can do all things through Christ which strengtheneth me."*
> **Philippians 4:13**

Everyone is going to go through things in life. Some of us have lived a trying life. Some of us have lived through the depths of ugliness, and yes, some of us find a way to still see the beauty in that ugliness.

What have you been through lately? That answer changes each and every day. Expect it to. In fact, it may just change each and every moment. The one constant in change is when you lean on God, He can (and will) give you the strength to get thru it.

Part of life is loss. Yes, we all experience loss, yet it is how we deal with it the shows our heart, where we are in life, and our character. When I got the news of Bryan's wreck....I remember my Pastor, Dave Baker, telling me to remember this phrase...."God's grace is sufficient."

Granted when I look back, I can barely even remember those first few weeks or how I actually functioned. You probably have experienced some of those type of moments as well. Our hearts and minds protect themselves by living in the "I'm okay" world. We put on our "blinders," our rose colored glasses, our fake smiles, and just go for it. I am sure the only way I survived those first few weeks was through God's grace. That is the only explanation.

I think I was more in shock; talking and just making movements. I do remember re-saying "God's grace is sufficient" over and over again, while praying for God to help me make the right decisions. I remember repeating this phrase over and over in my mind, each time focusing on a different word in the phrase, and that also seemed to help. GOD'S grace is sufficient. God's GRACE is sufficient. God's grace IS sufficient. God's grace is SUFFICIENT.

Each time I focused on a different word, I would feel the significance of that word even more with it's meaning. Focusing on God. He has the power and does give life, as well as take it away. Everyone has a time-line in this world, and we are all here for an appointed time, and like it or not, we must understand that and know and try to live life and find and serve our purpose while we are here. When I focus on grace, it reminds me of His wonderful grace and to be thankful and grateful for all the things He has given me. When I focus on the word is, it reminds me His grace IS sufficient, it absolutely is, if I allow it, I have that choice, to allow it to be sufficient or not, it is, but it is my choice, my free will, whether I allow it. Sufficient, when I focus on that word, yes, it is sufficient, it is enough, when I don't think I have anything else, and sometimes we don't, His grace is sufficient, it is all I need.

"Happy [is] the man [that] findeth wisdom, and the man [that] getteth understanding."
Proverbs 3:13

Many years ago, when I was studying to be successful, I noticed something spectacular. I noticed that every millionaire who I ever met, READ, a lot. That had to be a common bond. I have been very blessed to be personal friends and spend time personally with many millionaires and billionaires. In talking with all, I found they all read a lot, personal development, personal or business success, always learning and reading more to develop more. Most read on an average a book a week. Most average people, read a book a year or sometimes less. I really believe there is some significance in that. I learned this in my early twenties, and I have read an average of a book a week since then. I have books in almost every room in my house, in my car, in my briefcase, etc. So no matter where I am, if I have even five minutes, I can grab a book and read a few pages. I also have tons of audio books, training, the Bible on audio, and some good music on my phone, and whenever I get into my truck, it is set to automatically sync with my truck radio system and start playing to teach me while I drive no matter where I am going. Reading expands the mind and shows us the value of a choice. If you know all of your options, we can know and understand the choices we are making.

And, one book they all had in common, yes, all of the millionaires I met, read their Bible. Of course, they read other books. They were learning. I figured there was a reason, and I wanted to be successful - both in money, and in happiness (and in life), spiritually and emotionally.

Keeping this information in mind, I chose to be a reader; I never was one younger. Despite the fact I was a straight "A" student, I just didn't care to read. Opening my Bible wasn't the challenge. It felt every time I opened my Bible, I was SO tired! I found audio-bible.com, and I started to read my bible while listening to it.

Oh my goodness! I found I got a TON more out of it than I ever was able to just reading. I also found on my books, if I read just 1-2 pages at a time, 2-5 times a day — I would retain more out of what I read, and I got to where I was reading about a book a week. Now, I have done that now for over 20 years. I remember Zig Ziglar teaching the more you read, of good things, can be an equivalent to a college degree, bachelors, masters, etc … (so not sure which degree I would be on by now lol). I still read every single day, and I love to read now.

A psychologist, William James, once said, "The greatest discovery of any generation is that a human can alter his life by altering his attitude." It is a choice on having a good attitude or a bad attitude. When you have a good attitude, you will be more happy and find more things to be grateful for.

"Rejoice evermore."

1 Thessalonians 5:16-18

God commands us to be happy and rejoice. He loves us so much that He asks us to rejoice. To have joy. Being happy is a CHOICE. You can choose to focus on the negative, or you can CHOOSE to find something to be thankful and grateful for - and simply be happy. A little effort can go a long way. Simply trying to be happier, can actually elevate your mood and well-being. Listening to the right kind of music can help too. Listening to light and happy music can lift your spirits.

After Bryan was killed, I remember thinking, about being in my early 40's, and how, if I lived to be 105, that would be OVER 50 YEARS without him! How would I ever live 50 years alone?

Now, I had a choice when I read a card someone sent to me, with a poem in it - titled, "He is gone." When you read the words "he is gone," the dread that could enter your mind and your heart. Yet this poem shared a beautiful thought. I could choose to be sad for the next 20 plus years we will not have together, or I could be happy for the 20 years God gave him to me. Instantly, in that moment, I chose to focus on the many years we had together and to not any longer focus on the years we would not be together in the future.

For one day we will see each other again. And, 50 years will seem like a blink of the eye when I am dancing with him for eternity. I know that I am happy for him and his time in the Kingdom, walking the streets of Gold.

> *"And we know that all things work together for good to them that love God,*
> *to them who are the called according to [his] purpose."*
> **Romans 8:28**

This verse, I will tell you, I had trouble with how people used it. Mainly because some people phrased it to me, "God only does things for good, and God doesn't take away."

And right after Bryan was killed, it seemed my business "took off" even more, I had already been quite successful my life and business, and now, I was being blessed even more financially as well as in many other areas, so I was very thankful and grateful. Yet at the same time, I felt guilt. I felt like "Bryan had to die in order for me to be more successful."

Sharing this with a friend, they said to me, "No guilt; because God is blessing you. He is blessing you because you have been faithful. There is absolutely nothing wrong with that. Be thankful for it, allow the experience, and share and help others along the way, to see as you do."

I took some of the comments as, "God only does things for good" — well how do you tell a woman, who just lost her husband that? How could taking my husband be a good thing? And you continue by saying, "God doesn't take away."

Well, then, what does He do? Granted, I was not mad at God, and I know everyone has a "time to die." but this comment did not make sense to me at all. Frankly, it was hurtful when I thought about it. You can do your best to justify that the people telling me to focus on Romans 8:28, they loved me, and did not mean to tell me anything hurtful, but it just bothered me. When I found out that it was said to some of my kids, as they mentioned the same to me (even though I had not mentioned to them about the same comments made to me). In their questions, I didn't know how to respond to them, because I didn't know myself.

The more I studied and the more I prayed, the more I "chose" to "allow" that comment "God does take away" because He does. We may not like the reason, or think it is in our best interest, or whatever, but God has His reasons, and we must learn to trust in whatever His decision is for us, and find the why behind it, and how we can use that to help us walk through our own steps in those new shoes He gave us to walk in, and also then in turn help others to walk through them as well.

The most important thing to remember here is the Bible says we are to trust Him period, which I do. Of course, I still may not understand it, but I can choose to "not be happy about the situation, per se," but I CAN be happy in spite of the situation. By choosing to be happy, I have the amazing opportunity to look toward the future for what God DOES have for me. He will/can have GOOD for me and will work it together for God, if I love God and stay called to what I am supposed to be doing, He will bring things into my life that will be good.

> *"Rejoice in the Lord alway: [and] again I say, Rejoice."*
> **Philippians 4:4**

Once again — God commands us to rejoice — to be happy. Joy is internal. Happiness is external. You can show happiness to others. You can be happy because you went on vacation. But what happens when the vacation ends and you go back to work? You can show JOY, which shows from inside, and your whole ambiance shows to others, that is true happiness, when it is not just external, but also exudes from you internally.

God created us with five senses. Let each sense experience joy and true happiness everyday.

You can make the choice to be in atmospheres and around other people that will increase your probability of happiness. Make personal growth one of your top priorities in your life. When you do this, and value truth, you will find more happiness. Reprogram your beliefs and values if needed. None of us are required to live with the same from when we grew up or how we were raised if that does not fit for our best interests. We can make a choice for change for better at any time in our life, at any age.

Thinking about many of the cancer success stories I read. Once diagnosis took place, individuals took action in their own lives. They turned a switch. A JOY switch. People became happy as they blocked out all negative. Instead of watching the negativity on TV, they watched comedy dvd's, and they read happy stories only allowing things to enter their ears, eyes and mind that is positive.

Keep the law and you will be happy. The basis is simple; I teach my kids you do right, because it is right to do, not because of what the rules are, or what someone else is doing, or not doing, because it will come back to you. Some people call it the boomerang effect, or karma, but it is the basic principles of the universe which God created. When my children understood that when you do what is right, you will be able to lay your head on your pillow at night and rest peacefully. That is internal happiness. That is joy.

"I think myself happy, king Agrippa, because I shall answer for myself this day before thee touching all the things whereof I am accused of the Jews:"

Acts 26:2

Happiness is a CHOICE — you CHOOSE to do it, in spite of your circumstances.

We choose to be happy when we live life with an attitude of gratitude! When you look at a baby, what is there natural state? Bliss. Babies, toddlers, small children seek to find bliss. Even as adults, we desire bliss, but we let the life we have lived get in the way. We get to a place when we feel don't deserve happiness because of the mistakes.

When Peter was going in front of the king, (And you know, the king had the power to say "off with your head" just because he felt like it!) Paul said "I think myself happy." He CHOSE to think happy and think positive despite the trials he faced.

No matter what trials you are going through now, or what trials you may face in the future, you have a choice on how you react to them. You have a choice to be happy, and grateful and thankful for other aspects or situations in your life.

Implementing thankfulness and gratitude is a scientifically-backed way to increase happiness and it is completely within your control to choose to be more grateful. Grateful people tend to appreciate the simple pleasures. Pursue happiness. Find happiness. Find gratefulness. Find success.

Pursuing happiness not only leads to more happiness, but also to success.

> *"Behold, we count them happy which endure.*
> *Ye have heard of the patience of Job,"*
> **James 5:11**

Job went thru some trials and fires, didn't he? James tells us that all good things come from above. So we know that God didn't DO it, but He did ALLOW it to happen when Satan asked God. God allows us to go through trials so we can turn to Him. If we never know hurt, we will never understand the peace only He can offer!

Despite of all the trials, Job kept the faith. And, then, God blessed him, twice as much, the Bible shares with us. What we must understand, he didn't get his first kids "back". I am sure there were heart breaks and gut wrenching thoughts in there. In the hurt, he was given a chance to have happiness again because he had joy - always. Being blessed has nothing to do with "getting back" what we lost. Being blessed has everything to do with our attitude in each and every moment, to give of ourselves even when we don't think we can. God gave Job more kids, which still blessed him, and he was able to love, he was able to live successfully. The Bible says "We count them happy which endure." And Job counted himself happy always and endured each trial Satan put him through.

How about you? What trials have you endured?

I know people have told me before, "How do you stay so happy with _____?" (fill in the blank with every fire I have walked through.) We all go through things, and while I try to not ever dwell on them, I am being more transparent and talking about several personal in this book, not to ask for sympathy, but to show, how, yes, even though some see me as successful, which I am and thankful and grateful for that, also I, like everyone else in the world, go through things, and how some of those things, I have chose to make the choice to find ways in which to be thankful and grateful rather than focusing on the negative, and while God chose to allow me to go through some of these, I am trying to honor Him, by sharing some, and hopefully helping someone, as they walk through the shoes God gives for them to wear.

Same thing, happiness is a CHOICE, and God says we are to be thankful and grateful for what we have, and to DWELL on things of GOOD rapport. We are not to think and dwell or whine about things we don't have. We aren't even supposed to dwell on things we had in the past that we no longer have. Does that wake up your emotions? People who on purpose cultivate a positive mindset perform better in the face of challenges. We are all going to always face challenges in life, so why not on purpose, cultivate that mindset towards positivity and happiness to be able to better face those challenges in the future?

There is a difference in missing someone and loving them still even though gone. I love and miss Bryan every day, and yes, sometimes still cry when I think about it. I feel hurt and tears when I think of those who have gone before me: my Grandpa, my Father-in-law, my kids Grandpa and Grandmother who was a part of our lives so many years, and my Mom, as well as so many others.

Feelings and tears happen, and there is nothing wrong with that at all. Yet God doesn't expect us to STAY there, or DWELL there. Yes, we can miss them, and yes even cry for them, or even desire to see them. Then (not move on, because it is not necessary to do that, (unless you want to or feel God says to) but it IS important to move FORWARD and on for God, yourself and others, and get your heart and mind back "happy".

The best way to move forward is to be thankful and grateful for the blessings God has bestowed upon you. And, that is a choice we all must make. Be ready to make it because you are worth it. Life is a choice. Choose wisely. Choose honestly. Choose consciously. Choose happiness.

Whether you want to believe it or not, you are responsible for how happy you are. I am responsible for how happy I am. There is a lot of power in that thought. We get to choose all the shots to our own happiness.

Nature is a perfect example of this. Think about the saying, "Make like a tree and leaf!" We know this is a play on words. But in all things, we can find meaning. God's magnificent creation was done on purpose. There is meaning in each and every part of what God created. Nature is a parable of our own lives.

Trees and Leaves. Leaves and Trees.

The trees know God created them to shed their leaves. They must shed in order to move forward. In order to bloom. They let go of their leaves in joy, and God blesses them with beautiful new blooms. He doesn't give them the old blooms. He gives them new blooms to bless the birds, to bless the bees, and to bless us. The tree doesn't dwell and whine and cry over its lost leaves. It simply moves forward, so it can let go, allow new leaves to come into its life, and bloom again.

Are you ready to choose Joy and Happiness? Yes! Get ready to bloom!

> *"Do you really want to be happy? You can begin by being appreciative of who you are and what you've got."*
> **—Benjamin Hoff, The Tao of Pooh**

Find Happiness in Who You Are — in being yourself. To find happiness in who you are, ask yourself, "Who am I?" Take ownership of who you are and know you were created to be you just as you are … imperfect? Yes. But, perfectly imperfect. Perfect in your imperfections.

Find the most compassionate place of your heart. Never should we compare journeys with another. Why? We can never fully understand what another person is going through even when our journeys are similar; they are never the same, we all have different shoes we walk through this glorious life with. What is "bad" for you may be a catastrophe for someone else. What is okay for someone else may be life changing for you. We all have different ideas of good, bad, right, wrong, life-changing experiences.

What we must do is hold compassion for others, even when we are experiencing down in the dumps, not achieving our goals, feeling yucky kind of days. Compassion is our compass in how we treat others. And, it is the passion we seek life and relationships with.

Compassion always leads to happiness because we feel good about who we are, what we were able to do, and we want to continue to live, share, and be. You are a human being designed for compassion. You can give comfort and grace, empathy and healing to others. You never know, your one step of compassion - where that may lead, and what it may mean to someone else, along a same or similar journey. Let it shine in you and through you. That is a choice.

Chapter Number 2

Eating
We have the choice as to what we put in our mouth

Every day we make choices as to what we put into our mouths. The words "no one wants to hear," right? Yet, these are words that are so important to us as a whole person. Us, and only us, have the say so in what goes into our mouths (just like what comes out!). What we choose to put into our mouth and into our bodies It makes a huge difference in how we feel, many times on our attitude with others, and has effects on our overall health.

Talking with a friend just yesterday, she shared with me how when she drinks something with caffeine in it, she is more agitated easier, feels more stressed, and her overall mood is not as peaceful as when she simply chooses to not put things in her mouth that have caffeine in them.

My mom was a certified reflexologist, licensed massage therapist, and nutrition consultant. You could say (and I do) I was raised quite health-conscious. Even after I was married and raising children, I, of course, always wanted and tried to feed them better choices, to stay healthy; when the kids were smaller and we went through different financial stages in life that many families do, I knew the choices I made would affect them for the rest of their lives.

I was very blessed and thankful and grateful, that with every child, I was able to lose the weight I gained with them, and get back to my size 2/4 clothes.

The first time I saw a change was several years after my youngest was born, Bryan, my husband at the time and children's father, had hurt his back with a mixture of football in high school, being on the police department, wearing 50 pounds of extra equipment, and going from sedentary in the police car, to running through projects, jumping fences chasing someone, to breaking up fights, to weight-lifting and body building. He was in excruciating of pain and chose to have a surgery the doctors assured him would help.

But it didn't, and in fact, he got much worse. The more pain he was in the more doctors simply gave him pain pills to manage the pain , which led to sleeping pills to sleep, and other pills to help him wake up and get going, and yet more to relax muscles in his joints. The effects caught up with him and his body, and he had to leave his job due to the pain.

When Satan wants you, he goes after you with full force. The roller coaster ended up causing addictions, and I had to get a job, which enabled us to have insurance for him and our family.

Thankfully, I found a job I was able to do from home — answering phones for a company — but sitting 6 a.m. until midnight working to cover and try to keep up with our bills, especially our medical bills, and our situation; led to financial, emotional, spiritual, physical, stress in my life, which showed up physically in me, as gaining 70 pounds.

Within a few years, my income from my businesses got better, Bryan had went away to a year long Bible school and graduated early at 9 months. He came home and was doing so much better. His plans were to go back to the police department, although there was not an opening until July 2013. He stayed the course and decided to drive for the local FedEx that needed a driver for a few months.

I thought, with much stress relieved, the weight would just fall off, but it didn't! Even though I was eating pretty healthy. I didn't understand, I rarely ever ate deserts, didn't have a sweet tooth, I cut out most everything I knew to change, got some exercise, and was not seeing results, despite many things I tried, plans and products.

February 2, 2013, Bryan was killed on the job due to black ice. There was 157 wrecks that day, and his was the only fatality.

I was left with more choices. I need to take a deep breath, even now, as I think about more choices, with these yet, another pair of new shoes to learn to walk in.

A few months later, after winning some awards with one of the companies I represent, I became convicted about my weight. It was very honoring and a blessing to win the award, but when I got home and saw the pictures I cried about the way I looked. I felt depressed that I had let myself get to that point, but yet on the same note, I knew I mostly ate low carb, pretty healthy, rarely snacks or deserts, etc. I just did not get it!

But I resolved, my kids lost one parent, and I know health is important, and I was going to do all I could to make sure that my kids never had to go through losing their other parent, especially if I could help it regarding my health. My choice. My decision. My life.

"Do you not know that your bodies are temples of the Holy Spirit, who is in you, whom you have received from God? You are not your own; you were bought at a price. Therefore honor God with your bodies"

1 Corinthians 6:19-20

No one forces you to put that food or drink into your mouth, whether it is a good decision food or a bad consequence food. The trouble is that we sometimes put in in our mouth before we even think about it. After we eat it, too late, and then many times the regrets happen. We need to retrain our brain to think first and eat later. (Remember Chapter 1 about those decisions? Thinking about it now leads to less stress later!)

We are meant to treat our bodies like a temple. Are you treating your body like a temple? Ask yourself some of these questions: Do I really need that? Is that piece of cake, or whatever worth the calories? Just that little piece has a lot of calories. And once I eat it, will I feel better or will I regret it? What is my true motive at this moment? Am I truly hungry or just am I just craving something that I shouldn't have? Is it beneficial or detrimental to my health? That is a lot of questions about which we must think.

If we want to truly resolve and get healthier, we must answer those to ourself daily before we just flippantly put something in our mouth. We must slow our "habits" down. Those habits of licking the peanut butter off the spoon after making a little one a PB&J or eating a snack out of a bag instead of pouring it into a bowl. (This is a dangerous one because when we eat a "cheat" snack out of a bag, we have no idea how much we are actually putting into our mouths! We are showing our bodies that we are making a choice not to care.)

While asking ourselves the questions above, take a moment to write down the answers. Even write down the food you are eating. This gets us to see the food we are choosing to put in our mouths. This also allows us to see the good, the bad, the ugly of the decisions we are making when it comes to food.

Many people believe they have tried everything yet nothing seems to bring about desired changed in their lives. Do you feel like that sometimes?

I felt the same way. I rarely ever ate desert, and also rarely ever ate pasta, chips, bread, etc. So eating pretty healthy, many salads, usually organic proteins and greens, like 80-90 percent "on plan" as they would say, and even walking a few miles every day, I still was not seeing the results I desired.

When I decided to be 100 percent on plan, I started to see results. I had tried several "plans" out there, as well as several companies supplements plans too, and none produce any results for me. It wasn't until I finally just went 100 percent tweaking a plan just for me; it worked. I saw results!

It was hard. I knew I had to be diligent if I wanted to see the results I desired along with achieving the optimum health I wanted to assure me and my children I intended (and wanted) to be here and be healthy to be here for my kids and (one day) my grandkids.

My plan was pretty simple. No eating before 11 a.m. or after 7 p.m., with some exercise in the morning, and about 10 ounces water every hour. Why would I choose to not eat before 11 a.m.? When you do not eat in the morning, before a workout, your body is like in a "fasting" mode, from not eating all night. Then only drinking water actually allows you to get about 3 times the effect out of any workout you do in the morning before putting food into your stomach.

I chose walking. And, I would simply just walk 3-5 miles each morning. Then when I would eat, it was always very simple (no creams/sauces as many of those have fattening things or even sugar in them). Each plate/meal was a simple protein such as: wild caught alaskan salmon, organic chicken breast, or 96 percent lean ground beef. Then, I would add my vegetable: (always green) broccoli, asparagus, green peas or green beans. As a "treat" if I was eating out, I would get a salad with grilled chicken breast or grilled shrimp, and a light vinaigrette. I was drinking about 150 ounces water every day, I didn't drink anything but water. (Water is life.)

Occasionally, when working with clients much of the day I would forget to eat…..That was honestly one of my biggest problems, was not eating enough, not that I was eating the wrong things or too much, but then when I would eat, my body would freak out and think it needed to save every bit, because it might not get that nourishment again soon.

When I stuck to the plan 100 percent, I was losing about 10 pounds a month. It was hard to stay so diligent, very hard! It was worth it when I finally started seeing results!

I know many people that would follow a plan similar, and only 80-90 percent and see great results, but for me, I didn't. It wasn't until I finally stuck to it completely that I actually started to see results. Going through it, from the time I started, I had about 70 pounds to lose, so it was really hard to stick to 100 percent seeing results so slowly, and dis-heartening when I would see others follow anything close, but still only at 80 percent and get better results than me, or so I thought. But, same thing, we all have our own "shoes," right?

You know we many times tend to be our own self-worst critic, and I work on that every day. Looking at someone we admire, thinking they are better than us, or they deserve better because … Not true! Don't ever let your mind tell you that lie! I don't know if you struggle with that, but I did. See yourself as worthy and the choices you make in what you put into your body will change. See yourself as worthy and the choice in how you present yourself to the world changes. You are worthy. Always.

I made a choice to be diligent.

Now, I wasn't perfect, with all the traveling I do, and speaking all over the country at different events, I would end up either caving to a Starbucks Frappachino one morning, or maybe having some pasta at a meal that was being provided to me. But, I would get back on plan 100 percent the following day and take that as my one cheat for the month. I knew if I did any more than that — I would not see results.

Results is what we are all constantly striving to see, to hear, to feel.

It took a long time to complete, sometimes it seemed like forever! Some months I would end up having more than one cheat … and many times it was hard to be diligent, I fought the thoughts in my head all the time, well this one bite, then I will get back on plan. If I am at this event and they gave me this food, I need to be respectful and eat it. Or the thought, "Just this once won't hurt." And, of course, "I paid good money for this food, and there are people in the world starving that would love this I need to be grateful and eat it." Oh, the excuses and all the lies we can tell ourselves (and do tell ourselves to make things seem or appear as want), mixed with just that little bit of truth to make us feel guilty.

There is a great unknown; it is called tomorrow. The only way to see what it holds is to wake up, open your eyes, get out of bed, and go for it!

Now, that I have finally reached my goal in my fitness areas, I am so happy, grateful and thankful, that I finally chose to stick through it all and get back to the health and weight that I desired, and is best for my body.

I found a plan that worked for me. I could find the plan because I made a choice to see what I needed. Me. I took a few moments just for me and my health and my life. I knew my strengths and the areas I need to improve. It is imperative you know your areas of strengths and where you need/desire improvement because there are so much information at our finger tips, and it can be overwhelming. Right here in this moment we are taking away the choice of feeling overwhelmed. We are getting right to it because the right now is about you. What do you need to feel, look, sound, and be healthier?

Maybe you currently choose to eat too much at one time. Make the decision to use a smaller plate … resulting in less food on your plate!

Maybe you are currently putting too much soda into your mouth and body. Try substituting one glass of water for one soda over a couple a days and then substitute another one until you are only drinking water!

Maybe you don't know exactly when you are hungry. Many times our body knows exactly what we need, but we don't listen. We kind of feel hungry so we vote to eat food instead of drinking water. In many cases we are dehydrated, but we view it as hunger. If we are drinking enough water, then the choice to not eat all day long becomes easier because our bodies are getting what they need. This helps eliminate cravings!

Worried about not feeling full and then choosing to snack throughout the day? During meals add more fiber-rich foods and high-proteins. You will stay fuller longer! Making the choice to stick to healthy foods easier.

Maybe you already eat pretty healthy, but you deal with "brain fog." Widows many times call this "widow brain." Haha! Truth, sometimes we need to have that extra clarity in our life. Sometimes you may lack focus after meals. Choose to read the labels on your foods. Are you eating "healthy" processed foods? Trade out that processed health food for real fruits and veggies. And, even consider the option of filling half of your plate at meal times with fruits and veggies. God gave us plants. Each plant, each fruit, each veggie has particular minerals and vitamins our bodies need and crave. Give your taste buds and adventure by trying and choosing new foods. Create some tantalizing treats!

Maybe you are eating too often. I found if I allowed time for the foods to properly digest in my body before putting another bite into my mouth that helped as well. What worked for me was waiting three hours between meals. From the time I took my last bite from my last meal, having a three hour time span, before I took the next bite from my next meal. If you snack too often, your body doesn't have time to go through the full digestion process before it has to start over on the new you gave it, stopping it in its tracks, not being finished with the last part.

Do you have a busy life? A family with a "drive-through" schedule. Take ownership of your schedule. Make time to plan your meals. When you plan you meals, you are less likely to eat in a drive-through or just eat whatever you can get your hands on. It is amazing what choosing a plan does for your mind and your body!

Kids are picky eaters? Or, maybe, you are the picky eater! (Haha!)

Most of us won't start on this healthier journey because we evaluate the journey as "too hard." Eating healthier doesn't have to be complicated. The cornerstone of a healthy diet can be as simply as the choice to replace processed food with real whole food when possible. Eating food that is as close as possible to the way nature made it can and will make a huge difference to the way you think, look, and feel.

When God designed Adam and Eve's bodies in the beginning, He designed them to only eat raw the fruits, vegetables, and nuts found in the garden of Eden. In the Bible, people did not start eating meat until after the flood.

Not saying or getting into the argument of whether you should eat meat or not, granted I was vegetarian for twenty-five years, and still got fat, due to other stressors in my life. Just because you are vegan or vegetarian doesn't mean you are making the healthiest wisest choices in those areas. Vegans can technically still eat potato chips, candy, and vegan cookies (sugar)!

I choose to eat healthy, lean and wild caught if possible meats now, but just making a point on how our bodies were first designed and created. You have to think about and pray about the best choices for you and your family. But the closest form to the way God made them is always best.

Remember our bodies are temples. We must choose to treat them as such because we are worthy. We are worthy in His eyes. We must choose to be worthy in our own eyes.

Choose to see it. Choose to fuel life in your body. Say it now, "I am worth it! I will treat my body like a temple!"

Now, do it!

Chapter Number 3
Fitness
We have the choice to get on that treadmill

Do you have an alarm? What goes through your mind when it wakes you from a deep sleep? Are you one of those who hits the "snooze" button? Or, do you jump out of bed ready to start your day? No matter if you are a morning person or a night owl, when your eyes open, you have the choice of how you want to start the day. What frame of mind your day will begin?

Monday through Thursday I set my alarm for 6:30 a.m., and I choose to get up and walk on my treadmill for about an hour and a half. This time allows me to walk about three miles. It may be at a slower speed, but I am getting it done! And, being a multi-tasker, I have created a treadmill desk enabling me to work on my laptop while I walk as well as talk to clients (if I need to during that time). This is also the perfect time for me to get my personal motivation and personal development time on! I am usually reading or listening to something positive to uplift me, help me in my personal or business life, and/or motivate me. Choosing to start my day positively, I am preparing my body and mind for what I am asking it to do all day long.

Did you realize that as you are reading, right now, someone just made the DECISION that will effect the quality of their life — in a positive or negative way?

Before we can talk fitness, let's understand what fitness actually is. One of the definitions of fitness is: "the quality of being suitable to fulfill a particular role or task." Think about what fitness means for a moment. Have you prepared your body for the role, for the tasks, you ask it to do?

When you make the decision to get on the treadmill, turn in on, and actually begin to walk (whatever the treadmill is for you) to prepare your body for the role and tasks you ask of it, take the time to have these in place. It will help you bring your goals to realization (not just a dream or a thought).

1. **Decide on your fitness goals.**

2. **Focus on your fitness program bringing one additional thing to your life (beside the obvious of better fitness/better health).**

3. **Picture (have a picture, make a picture, vision board) how your training program will intersect and benefit your everyday life.**

4. **Look at your schedule. Know how your training will fit into your schedule. Otherwise, you will never get out of bed.**

Hitting your snooze button or jumping out of bed to get on your treadmill (whatever your treadmill may be) is a life altering decision. The results of your decision today will be seen for month and years to follow. Everything in life starts with a simple decision. What voice will you make today?

Working out in any capacity requires commitment. It also requires your brain to be on board with your decision. Your brain will control your body's effort in this.

> *"He giveth power to the faint; and to them that have no might he increaseth strength. Even the youths shall faint and be weary, and the young men shall utterly fall: But they that wait upon the Lord shall renew their strength; they shall mount up with wings as eagles; they shall run, and not be weary; and they shall walk, and not faint."*
>
> **Isaiah 40:29-31**

God will help you, and you will be rewarded for all your fitness efforts. Especially when you do it in His efforts, not just merely for vanity or selfish reasons. Granted there is nothing wrong with wanting to look good for yourself, or your spouse etc. But put your trust in God and He will always guide you.

Create a workout plan that works for you. A gym? If you are on that treadmill and the walls feel like they are pushing in like a tidal wave, it is time to change the pace. Maybe you should just go walking around your neighborhood. Do what you know inspires you, not drudgery task. Do you need to keep it interesting (not doing the same routine everyday)?

I try to add other activities throughout the week, sometimes I will go to the gym in the evenings, or go hiking on the weekend, etc. I have found what interests me. You need to find what interest you. And, then let it work for you!

Also, I know me, and I know if I don't get it done first thing in the morning, many times my day gets booked with clients' needs or family's needs I need to take care of. There it is! Before I know it — it is midnight and time for me to go to bed to start the next day. Choosing to make it important, I try to make sure I get it over with first thing in the morning.

Remember, when you work out first thing in the morning, you have "fasted" all night long without eating, and if you go ahead and work out before breakfast and before drinking anything but water, you will get about three times the effect from your work out than you would have if you work out later in the afternoon or evening. That is huge! I would much rather get three times the effect for better for my time!

Simply walking also has some amazing health benefits. Just some of those benefits are improving your brain's mood, relieving back pain, reduce your hips, lowers the risk of blood clots in your legs, lowers blood pressure, lowers the risk of heart attack, strengthens your arms, tightens abdominal muscles, keeps your knee joints healthy, can increase your self-esteem, tone your muscles, reduce stress, increase energy, boost endorphins, limit sickness, reduce risk of osteoporosis, improves balance, strengthens legs, improves heart health, and many more!

I use a Fit Bit tracker to measure my steps. Personally, I try to get 10,000 steps in each day. I work from home and own a few businesses, which all involve being on a computer or meeting with clients. This can lead to a lot of sitting if I am not careful. I absolutely love what I do — it isn't really work for me so I devote many hours to building my businesses (and helping others). This devotion can easily get caught up, and before I realize it, I have sat way too long.

Keeping this in mind and understanding what works for me, I made the bold decision to get up when that alarm clock buzzes and get on the treadmill. Decision have consequences — good or bad — and the decision to get up and walk first thing in the morning, starts off my day with about 5,000 steps. Yes, 5,000 steps right off the bat. Throughout the day I will get in the rest. Sometimes I can check in the evening, and maybe go for a nice walk after dinner if I hadn't got close to my goal for some reason.

There are easy choices you can make to help you add more steps without taking too much time, especially if you don't have that gym time or treadmill at home.

"I can do all things through Christ which strengtheneth me."
Philippians 4:13

Nothing is impossible with God. We all have to look at our human limits. Depending on your age, health and abilities, set realistic goals for you to achieve but do not be too afraid to make lofty goals. Dedicate your workouts to Christ, see the difference that can make. If you are unhealthy and die, you won't be here to lead others towards Him. Trust in Him to help you and guide you, so you can do more for others while you are here on this Earth.

The first choice is park further when from the entrance to anywhere you go! Yes, don't look for that close parking spot; go ahead and park a little farther back. Your health will thank you. Then, when you arrive, take the stairs instead of the elevator.

While talking on the phone or waiting at an appointment, walk around the room. (The only negative consequence may be the trail you leave in the carpet!) When cooking that healthy dinner, walk around the kitchen.

If you watch TV, don't use the remote, get up and walk over to change the channel. Or choose to see your TV times as yoga, stretching, ab, or leg workout time. Yes, sit on the floor and start those sit-ups, inner thigh lifts, a few Warrior poses, and remember to stretch. You are getting your body moving and releasing the stresses of the day as well! Go on an after dinner walk with the family or your significant other (this walk can be romantic and produce other activities/exercise later that night!)

Take a break at work and go for a walk, this will also refresh your mind allowing you to focus on your work better when you return. March in place while brushing your teeth, curling your hair, putting make up on etc. Arrive to an appointment early? Don't sit in the waiting room, walk the room. Standing in line at the post office or store? Just bounce on your toes, working your calf muscles at the same time.

In life, the small things add up. Did you gain a significant amount of weight overnight? No, it was those small unhealthy choices you made finally adding up. Adding up in the form of pounds. Today is the day to reverse the effects of those choices. Yes, let's make the small decisions to healthier choices and a healthier you! The more small choices towards your good health and well-being every day, will show in better looks and feeling over time in your body over-all.

"What? Know ye not that your body is the temple of the Holy Ghost which is in you, which ye have of God, and ye are not your own? For ye are bought with a price: therefore glorify God in your body, and in your spirit, which are God's."

1 Corinthians 6:19 & 20

Give glory to God in everything. Yes, your workouts can even glorify God. You can pray while you walk, meditate while you swim, think and dwell on God's greatness while you work out in the weight room. If you are a music lover, get dancing/praising to some rocking worship music. God does ask that we sing and dance unto Him. He calls for us to be active. He opens doors, but it is our choices that get us to walk through the door. An open door is just an open door until you walk through it.

Now, if you have that treadmill in your house (dust it off and get walking), you can put your steps to better use. Set your treadmill incline one notch higher, this will help to increase your strength and improve muscle tone faster. They say if you weigh 150 pounds and walk 2 mph you will burn about 75 calories every 30 minutes. So, while that might not seem like a lot and it is a slow pace to be able to do other things, it is 100 times better than being sedentary on your computer desk chair or the sofa.

When I walk, I usually do 1.5 mph (I am only 5'2" so short legs; haha, yes I can laugh at myself!). Granted that is a slow walk for me, but if I need to talk to clients or type on my laptop, I still can at that rate, and I will do 2 hours, so that will give me about 5000 steps and about 300 calories. When I am not working and focusing on walking, I will do 2.5 mph (that is a pretty fast walk for me; 3 mph I am jogging) and I will try to do an hour at that when I am at the gym (this is the only time I ever watch tv, and I try to find something I can get interested in, something positive, or like I like to watch business ideas on Shark Tank for example, and then I do not focus on the time as much, which helps me).

Regardless, any walking or moving rather than being at your desk chair or on the couch is going to be helpful. My Apple watch has an option to ping my wrist every hour at ten minutes till, to remind me to get up and move for 10 minutes. I set my watch, so that way if nothing else, that one day I am working a lot on web based projects, it reminds me to get up and take a break. Oh, this break, how it also helps to make me more refreshed, in my mind and in my body. Making the choice to refresh my mind and my body, I get more done in that next hour than if I sat through that ten minutes and kept trying to work.

Where can you make healthier choices to get moving? Remember this: motion creates emotion.

When you are feeling down, get moving. When you are feeling stressed, get moving. When you are feeling blah, get moving. Our bodies are designed to move.

"A wise man is strong, yea a man of knowledge inscreaseth strength"

Proverbs 24:5

It's important to include strength training exercises as part of your fitness program. Not only will every day chores and other activities become easier, but you will also strengthen your bones. Try lifting weights, using stretch bands or cords, you can use kettle balls or medicine balls, or even doing some exercises that utilize your own weight, like dancing. My gym provides a body pump class once a week. The exciting part; it fits into my schedule most days. Bonus, I even found a lady to go with me. We can push each other to go each week, when one of us might not want as much.

"She girth her loins with strength, and strengtheneth her arms"

Proverbs 31:17

Again, the Bible tells us to sing and dance upon the Lord. Why? It is the action that draws us closer. We can feel him when we are enjoying praising him. I understand this may not be your belief. But, it is mine. And, it is proven that emotion and movement are linked. So, why not give it a try? You are worth it, remember.

Find something that makes you sing and dance. You may just find it strengthens you body as well as your soul. This choice to get moving may just inspire your next dream and be the first step to your next success. Something beautifully amazing happens when our bodies move and we make that choice to feel and be healthier. We glow! So, get moving. Let's glow together!

"I therefore so run, not as uncertainly; so fight I, not as one that beateth the air: But I keep under my body, and bring it into subjection: lest that by any means, when I have preached to others, I myself should be a castaway"

1 Corinthians 9:26 & 27

Don't do your exercise half-heartedly. Set some attainable goals, daily, weekly, monthly, yearly. Create your plan (this means you must write it down. You have an 80 percent greater chance of achieving your goals when you write them down versus those who just say them or think them). Once you have created your plan, it is time to execute it, to take action and make it happen. Choose to make it happen.

When our bodies are strong, it makes it easier to fight the battles of the mind and achieve true overall health.

Only you can make it happen. God has opened the door to a physically healthier you. The door is open, choose to get up, choose your shoes, and choose to walk through it. Choose this everyday. For everyday is a choice. Everyday is chance to choose differently, choose wisely, choose you!

Chapter Number 4

Health

We have the choice to listen to our body's needs

Have you ever been extremely busy, going non-stop, getting up early and staying up late? After a few days of this, your throat begins to hurt. your eyes burn, your head throbs. These are signs of your body begging you to listen!

When you were younger, how did you picture the later years of your life? Were you 100-years-old? Or you are only 65-years-old? Are you the 100-year-old still driving, water skiing, telling stories to his/her great-great grandchild of what it was like to live in our present? Or are you the 65-year-old who once dreamed of traveling the world, but at the time, you only travel down to the dining hall at your assisted living home?

Some of us cringe at the thought of getting older. As younger human beings, most think they don't want to get so old that they can't take care of themselves so they picture dying peaceful in their sleep at an "earlier" age. Yet, as we gain years, "older" keeps getting pushed further and further out. At twenty, thirty-five seems like ages and many moons away. It is old! Then, thirty-five quickly approaches and fifty is now old. Fifty-year-olds picture eighty as ancient. And feisty 80-year olds strive to make it to the big 100!

Shakespeare's monologue is his play *As You Like It* presents to us Jacques. Jacques is not your happy-go-lucky kind of guy. His monologue present as a poem in the mind of Shakespeare fans. All the World's a Stage is the "poem."

Jacques takes us through the seven stages of life. In his mind, we arrive and leave this world the same — a state of infancy and dependency.

How can you change this?

Everyone wants better health, right? When we listen to our body's needs, many times that is like prescribing for ourselves. But who knows us better than ourself? The doctor's walls, all show "practicing medicine."

Most doctors have not taken any classes on nutrition for the body, or very few hours. Now, don't get me wrong, I love a good doctor if I need one, for any area of my life, that is more knowledgeable than me in that area.

However, I choose not to run to the doctor for every little thing. I choose to listen to my body, if it may be a cold or sickness, and try to figure out and practice myself of what I need. If that doesn't work, or if I have broken a bone or something major, then of course, I am very thankful and grateful to have amazing knowledgable doctors by my side who can perform miracles that I could never imagine doing.

> "What? Know ye not that your body is the temple of the Holy Ghost which is in you, which ye have of God, and ye are not your own? For ye are bought with a price: therefore glorify God in your body, and in your spirit, which are God's"

1 Corinthians 6: 19-20

I have heard it preached and taught many times using this verse to talk about not smoking, not doing drugs, not getting tattoos or piercings (and I am not saying my opinion in this matter here - that is for you to go to God yourself, and figure out through your own discernment in what all areas of your life this would apply to).

Although it is rarely mentioned this verse with eating and/or fitness? I wonder why? Because we want to only teach about what we believe or we want to, rather than what the Bible says? Does the Bible mean only certain areas of our life? But others on this subject don't matter? If the Christians are unhealthy and dying, how can they be here to spread the gospel and reach other souls for Christ?

Wholeness. What does that word mean to you? What picture does it paint? How does it make you feel? Wholeness has two definitions. The first: the state of forming a complete and harmonious whole, and the second: the state of being unbroken or undamaged.

Wholeness is simply being complete, unbroken, and harmonious. What areas to you need to achieve wholeness?

Wholeness should be a word you associate immediately when you think about your mind and your body. They are connected, but we must be open to listen to ensure that they are working at their maximum potential. Remember, every single cell experiences each and everything you put your body through: negative emotions (anxious, sad, depressed, stressed), positive emotions (excited, happy, blessed), when you are starving yourself or eating for emotional fill, etc.

Your body may not be able to physically speak, it can express itself through reactions ... a chemical, hormonal reaction.

The longer it takes us to hear and listen to our bodies, the louder and bigger the message it gives us until we have to stop altogether.

So, what is the best way to listen to your body?

First and foremost, we must be quiet to hear properly. In any relationship, we must quiet our mind and our voice to hear what the other person is saying. Treat your body and mind as a relationship. This is the longest lasting relationship you will ever have. Treat it right!

"Whether therefore ye eat, or drink, or whatsoever ye do, do all to the glory of God."

1 Corinthians 10:31

If you feel that you are going 100 miles an hour, if you feel down, if you feel sick ... whatever you are experiencing, take a deep breath. It has been stated that when you are taking deep breaths, it is impossible for your body to feel stress. How cool is that?!?!!

Once you have slowed down enough to hear, you must be okay with what your body is saying to you. Yes, accept it. It is okay. We all go through hurts, pains, sadness, etc. When we try to deny our feelings or our body, we push it deeper down, cramming it in like we "pack" brown sugar into the cup when baking cookies. The harder we cram, the harder it is to get it to come out, and the sicker our bodies and minds can become.

We are scared to slow down. If you own your business or even if you work for someone else, we fear that if we slow down, we will lose money, business, our job. These losses can lead to further losses. Sometimes we feel we are stuck between a rock and hard place. Too many things riding on one choice. So, we keep cramming. We keep plugging away. Late nights. Early mornings. We only hear our fears instead of our bodies. Then that is what we attract more of. The same thing, this goes back to our thinking, getting thoughts in our head in the ways we want them to be. God says to "think on these things, as if ye have already received".

Choose right here and right now that is okay to slow down every once in a while. Long enough to hear what your body is telling you. These could mean keeping your job, growing your business, and making more money. Life is perspective. We must choose to see it in a positive light.

> *"And he said, My presence shall go with thee, and I will give thee rest."*
>
> **Exodus 33:14**

God even tells us to rest sometimes, our bodies need it. Our bodies heal while we rest. Our spirit can be restored while we rest.

F.E.A.R. False Evidence Appearing Real vs. H.O.P.E. Healing Opportunities Providing Excellence. Where will you put your focus? Your ear to listen. Listen to your H.O.P.E. side! It believes in your body!

Your body is actually on your side! Yes, it will value you even more when you listen to it.

In many cases, when stop and listen, we realize we must change our current patterns, moods, actions. Our minds and body need and crave spontaneity. Spontaneity helps unclog those blockages and packages we have created.

When we start to unblock, we can enjoy what our body wants and needs. For you, it may activities outdoors, reading a book, taking a nap, a special meal with a treat, eating right (with better choices), a massage, or even holding a loved-one's hand.

You will be pleasantly surprised. As when you learn to listen to your body, you will find the road to more self-confidence and less self-doubt. With more self-confidence, your actions will take notes. You are providing H.O.P.E. for you and your body.

You are leaving behind the overwhelming suffocation many feel in our insanely busy, anxious, and tense lives. H.O.P.E.

There are several ways we must listen to our body. When we are hungry/full, when we are tired, when we need to relax (slow down), when we need to get moving, and when we need time to heal.

Food again. Yes, the dreaded subject of listening to our bodies. Are we really hungry when we eat? Do we keep eating when we are full? Are we taking time to eat when we are hungry or starving ourselves?

Sleep is so important. More important than most of us "Americans" realize. Are you getting enough sleep? Our bodies are designed to rest, especially between the hours of 11 p.m. and 2 a.m. So get to bed! Put all electronics away one hour before bed. Make this choice and you will see vast important in your sleep.

Taking the time to relax and slow down ... even if it is just for a bit. Now, once you are relaxed it may be hard to get moving again. Many of us hate going "back to work" after an amazing vacation. We get so wrapped up in either relaxing or working. When we find the balance, we can move from one aspect to the other. Balance is healthy. Balance allows us to heal in all areas of our life.

"Return unto thy rest, O my soul; for the Lord hath dealt bountifully with thee."

Psalm 116:7

God tells us to rest. He made our bodies to work hard, but also to rest. It is important for us to do both. When awake, we should work to provide for ourselves, our family, etc. We should work hard to keep our body healthy and in shape. When it is time, we should also rest, and restore our soul.

Healing. Such a beautiful word with so many meanings. This is where most people struggle. They make the conscious decision to remain stuck where they are. Hurting works for them. They can eat whatever and whenever because it feels good. They can speak to anyone in any tone with any words because they hurt. They can lay depressed in bed because "they hurt." They can organize the house or keep going without thinking because it is an excuse of "I hurt."

Healing is a choice. Just as everything else is in this life. Healing takes effort. And, the reward of healing is beautiful. It feels peaceful — like a weight is off your back. It looks like joy and smiles. And, sounds as amazing as a baby's giggle.

When you listen to your body's needs, it can be called "prescribing for yourself." But who knows your body better than yourself? Granted this is not a comment to avoid doctors or anything else. You should always seek advice for anything health wise from your health care practitioner that you trust.

But you should listen to your body. Try to pay attention to what it is telling you. Many health issues come with warning signs first, that if we are paying attention, we can help alleviate problems in the long run.

Many of the biggest health issues are caused from what we eat and drink. Some say it is genetics, but usually it is really the genetics of the same ways of eating being passed down, causing the same health issues being passed down.

One of the things I have found over the years, is not even so much watching what you eat, although I do that a lot, but all the sugar in so much, even condiments. When you cut out sugar alone, you can help so many things. Cut out white and wheat flours too and helps even more.

I have been lucky to never had a "sweet tooth," but between ketchup and other condiments and sauces, creams etc, I still got plenty of sugar. I couldn't imagine where I would have been if I fought desert cravings too!

I cut out all white, wheat, and sugar for awhile. I found I still got so much until I actually started cooking more at home, using my own just seasonings. Of course, I maybe added a tiny bit of real butter! But, when I made this choice/decision, I started to see and feel even more amazing results. Sugar is everywhere in so-called healthy drinks. (I'm not talking about soda here … we all know the sugar issue in soda.) I am sharing with you about juices, smoothies, etc. So many have ingredients, that when you do research, you'd never put in your mouth; let alone your children's mouths. So, what do you put in your mouth to drink?

Water is essential to life. We cannot live with out. I did a test one day, I went to the health food store and bought some PH test strips. I bought almost every brand of water I could think. Using the PH strips, I came home and tested each brand of water.

Professionals say a higher PH is more healthy, a disease preventative, anti-aging properties liquid antioxidants can absorb faster, colon-cleansing properties, immune system support better hydration, which leads to healthier skin and weight loss. And, some say alkaline systems can prevent or lower your risk for cancer. I believe these potential benefits make it worth it for me to choose alkaline water! For me I am choosing health in my life.

Some purifiers out there ranging from all kinds of costs show PH levels and alkaline water. ("What is alkaline water?" you may be asking. It is simply this: Water naturally is alkaline when water passes over rocks such as in springs. As it passes over the rocks, the water picks ups minerals. The more minerals, the higher the alkaline level!) Each one is attempting to grow their business by selling filters. Knowing this information, I sought to test the water I was drinking because I desire an alkaline, healthy body. Every brand water I tested showed like a 2 to 3, which happens to be pretty acidic. Yes, every water I tested except for two: Evian and Fiji.

This showed me … my own two eyes … the difference in water. Watching the test, it was amazing to see the results and how much difference there was! Yes, not all water is the same.

Can you guess the brands of water I purchase now? You got it! Evian and Fiji are the only two brands of bottled water I buy now and will ever buy. When I am at home (not traveling), I use the filter on my sink by "Clean and Pure" because on the PH test, it tested high (alkaline) and so did my Samsung refrigerator water filter. I felt blessed by this. It is nice to be able to drink directly from my refrigerator and faucet. So I buy Fiji water, and I will refill the bottles sometimes from home when I can, but if I am out or traveling I only buy Evian or Fiji.

My Mom bought me a book many years ago. To this day, I still use. It is titled *Prescription for Nutritional Healing*. What I love about this book is you can look in this for what is ailing you, and it will give recommendations for vitamins, herbs, foods (and more) that might help. You can also look up specific vitamins to discover how it is important to your body, why you need it, and why you might be feeling a certain way if you need more.

Once again, **(PLEASE REMEMBER)** these comments are not intended to replace or go against any medical advice. If you have any questions, I would always highly recommend you check with your health care practitioner or doctor who you trust. Many times you can get a second, third, fourth opinion too. In the end, you are deciding for you and your family. This is important; it is your life, so do as much research as possible on both sides of the spectrum.

Sometimes medical attention is very necessary. When I had my gallbladder removed, I was very grateful and thankful I had an amazing, knowledgeable and caring surgeon to take care of me. When I delivered my children, I chose to have a midwife as well as a medical doctor — both who I absolutely love and trust with my health and my children's and am so grateful I had both by my side.

The key in both situations is I listened to my body, I knew it, and understood when something was good and when I needed medical attention. Knowing comes from listening.

You can't know someone without taking the time to listen to them and truly receiving the words they are saying. You will know "you" and your body when you take the time to listen.

If you were to pause here for a moment and listen, what would your body be telling you? Are you tired? Do you need to get up and move? Do you need a glass of water? Do you need a breath of fresh air? Go ahead pause for a moment. Close your eyes and simply listen.

Your body desires to live a fulfilling life. Maybe even one of adventure. A true journey before it reaches its earthly destination. Age isn't always a factor in our adventure; it is actually about how old your body feels. To live a life of adventure, we have to be strong enough to climb the mountains, surf the waves, run the paths, swim the streams, and patient enough to wait for the right moments and calm the storms.

Chapter Number 5

Business

We have the choice to do activities to help our business

When we own our own business, it can be hard sometimes to motivate and make ourselves do the things we need to in our business to help us move forward and propel us to new heights.

If we want to be successful, and if we want to make a difference in the world, we need to constantly re-evaluate ourselves consistently. Re-evaluating guides us our actions to the levels we want to achieve and better ourselves. We must make the decision to have a Game Plan, and then take action on it! Yes, we you got to be **S.M.A.R.T.!**

Be **S**pecific in your goals! **M**ake the Choice! **A**ct! Act Act! **R**ealize **R**esults! **T**ake everyday actions seriously!

In my businesses I run, I always write goals and have a business plan. I write them for every year, then break them down for every month, then weekly, daily, and even hourly. Yes, yearly goals comes first. You have to plan backwards!

> *"And whatsoever ye do, do it heartily, as to the Lord, and not unto men; Knowing that of the Lord ye shall receive the reward of the inheritance: for ye serve the Lord Christ."*
> **Colossians 3:23-24**

No matter whether you own your own business or you work for an employer, always work as if you were working for God. Hard work and diligence will always bring some type of profit. When we think about profit, many times we think money, but it can be about anything, really. Hard work in school is going to lead to better grades, more wisdom, a better job, more and better opportunities. Many people say, "I am going to do so and so", but then they never do that. Do what you say you are going to do. Don't be lazy.

I schedule everything on my calendar. Personal time as well as business time. So that way I know what I am doing at all times. Now, granted, I still allow for some flexibility in there as well. (We want to make sure we are living life, not just doing life!)

One, I stay on track with my business plans. **Two,** I know, understand, and have in front of me the action steps I need to reach the goals I desire. **Three,** you are telling yourself you have value, that you can do it, and that you will do it. Many get stuck when they fail to find value in who they, what they are meant to do in this life, and believing they can do it!

Make the Choice!

By making the choice to create a game plan, you understand the gifts you have to offer. And, know and make the choice to believe ... YOU ARE GIFTED!

Creating your plan can be simple (but not always easy). Decide on what you want. What do you feel good about? Decide the gifts you want to show the world. Who needs these gifts/talents? And, remember the "WHY" behind your business and your choices.

> "In any moment of decision, the best thing you can do is the right thing, the next best thing is the wrong thing, and the worst thing you can do is nothing."
> **Theodore Roosevelt**

Act! Act Act!

Once your plan is in place DECIDE to ACT. Don't let others doubt your plan. They aren't you and you aren't them. What works for you, well works for you. And DO IT.

> "In all labour there is profit: but the talk of the lips tendeth only to penury. The crown of the wise is their riches: but the foolishness of fools is folly."
> **Proverbs 14:23-24**

Realize Results!

We can all use building 'blocks" in our lives. My building blocks happen to be how I block my time. Yes, I create time blocks for everything, personal, business, and pleasure. The most important things go on my calendar first such as:

church, kids events, etc. Then, I add in my personal things and business things.

When creating these blocks, I must be dedicated to sticking to my time slots. Example: if I am working from home all day, I might allow three fifteen minute time slots for social media. (Social media can be a time-hole for some people so please careful, be intentional, set a timer if you must!)

In my fifteen minute time slot for social media, I will post a a few things for five minutes, then read, like and comment on posts for five minutes, and then check messages an reply for five minutes. Then, guess what! I am done. I turn it off. Log out. If I don't get all done everything I wanted during that time, I still log out. My time block is over, and I go onto my next task and fifteen minute time slot.

Time blocks can work for every task. To allow it to work, we must use it. Writing this book, and my first book I had wanted to for a long time, I felt like God was giving me things He wanted me to write, but I wasn't scheduling the time on my calendar. If it wasn't on my calendar, do you think it was getting accomplished? It was only when I put it on my calendar and then I committed to it, I completed the book and published it.

Same thing in our business, there are many activities to running a business. Some are money making activities, while others include: paperwork, follow up, and more "tedious" things (for those of use who would rather be out with people instead of at home behind a computer). The challenge: we need to make sure we have a balance.

Balance is a delicate process because we must take the necessary action to achieve it. Balance is key in everyone's life. And, as business owners, if we want to make sure we run our business the way we need to and succeed and produce more, balance (master our time) will lead the way.

Yes, in this crazy world of there is something to do every second of every day, there is entertainment and distractions 24/7, we seek to be masters of time. We can be so focused on making money, growing our business, we lose part of ourselves. We find ourselves spending too many hours in our business and neglect our personal friends and family or even ourselves.

> *"Your work is going to fill a large part of your life, and the only way to be truly satisfied is to do what you believe is great work. And the only way to do great work is to love what you do. If you haven't found it yet, keep looking. Don't settle. As with all matters of the heart, you'll know when you find it."*
> **Steve Jobs**

Take everyday actions seriously!

Because we seek to grow our business everyday, it is a constant state of growth. That state is a must for success. Every leader I know and very successful people learn every day. Constantly training, learning and studying to improve not only help your comprehension as well as skill and knowledge, but growth is crucial to your personal freedom.

When you own your own business, setting your personal finances in your business can be challenging. "It takes money to make money." Many times this slogan is true. Although, I do know some millionaires who went from zero to millions, because they just did not have any means for start up capital. It can be done, but it can be harder.

Running a business can You also have to know where to cut off a money drainer. Make sure you are keeping a salary to support you and your family. Also as becoming more successful, be sure to put some money away for investments, a rainy day, vacation, emergencies, etc. As you are building success in wealth, you can and will grow it further when you keep personal debt low or none (if you are able). Your quest to financial freedom will become a reality when you decide to choose these steps. You are prioritizing your money.

Prioritizing is critically important in business. Your to-do list can, many times, be never-ending, and even overwhelming. Setting up systems and delegating things can help you in your quest to being more diligent and better with your time. Prioritize your tasks, as many times the non-important things call for your attention more than the important things, so be careful in that area. Taking five extra minutes the night before, or first thing in the morning and making a list and prioritizing it can help you to stay on task to get more done through out the day.

If you don't take time to prioritize in your life, you are, in fact, making nothing important. Prioritizing creates freedom in your life. Freedom to see what you may not have previously *seen.*

> *"For I know the thoughts that I think toward you, saith the Lord, thoughts of peace, and not of evil, to give you an unexpected end."*
> **Jeremiah 29:11**

Prioritizing requires organization. I think about the movie, *Bruce Almighty*. As Jim Carey's character, Bruce, spends a few day looking through God's eyes, he develops an appreciation for what God goes through on a daily basis and even the moment-to-moment as Bruce hears the prayers of millions from around the world. To be able to hear each one and effectively answer them, he struggles to find a way to organize them.

From millions of post-its around the room to never-ending file cabinets, he finds email to be the best way to organize the prayers. Can you picture millions of post-it notes around your house as you write your to-do list? Your to-do list will keep getting longer, those post-it notes will keep growing until you take the necessary action to make things happen! Many times we don't prioritize because it means we have to create an effective organization plan. It locks our minds and our actions ... like pushing the pause button on the Blueray Player remote.

God may not reveal his entire plan all at once. I don't think we could handle it all at one time. We might see our shadow and run back into our groundhog holes. Every one of our steps (in life and in business) has already been designed and paved for us ~ even before we were even born. We know this because He gives us glimpses though visions and dreams. We do know and how he desires us to live a prosperous life.

We don't prioritize because we have chosen to see life through the a key hole. What can you see through a key hole? Only what it allows you to see.

Learning to see past the key hold means we must open the door. Success means you must **G.R.O.W.** — **G**aining **R**eliable **O**pportunities for **W**ealth. And, remember to grow, we must be **S.M.A.R.T**. in our business decision making skills.

When we seek to open new doors, ask 4 questions:

1) When I open this door, will it create new positive, productive opportunities?

New opportunities happen each and every day. But not every opportunity is positive and productive for you business. What is a productive and positive opportunity? One that leads to your goals. So, make sure you have your goals written down. And, have them posted where you can see them. When you are given the choice to open a door, ask yourself it it will guide you and take you closer to your next goal? Will it take you farther from your next goal? What is the risk factor? If it works out perfectly, will it take you closer, and if it does not work out perfectly, will it hinder you or put you behind further? Maybe you won't reach your goal, but maybe, just maybe you will take a few steps closer. And, every step forward is a step in an amazing direction!

Some opportunities may be smaller, quicker. Taking the time to learn how to recognize them is vital in your business and in your life. Why vital? There is power is each and every experience/opportunity. We can learn from everything.

2) When I open this door, will my company/product/brand/service be more recognized and visible to those who need and can use my services/product?

Growth doesn't happen in your business if you don't put yourself out to the world. When we make a choice in opening a new door, we want to make sure we are building our brand in a positive light to the right audience. One of the biggest mistakes business owners and entrepreneurs make is saying, "My audience is everyone." That is not true. Not everyone needs or wants your product or service. We must define and detail who can benefit from our products/services. Then, and only then, do we know how to market to that audience. We must get clear on who we want to attract and who we want to help.

When you shoot a gun, do you want bullets that splatter in 100 directions, or do you want a few or one, aimed in one direction for the most impact? When you define who your ideal customer or client is, you can set your arrows up to go in one direction and target just people that want to hear your message and need your product or service.

3) When I open this door, will it generate cashflow into my business?

Business growth shouldn't be measured just by cashflow, but it is a good sign of how well a business is growing/doing. Maybe the new door chosen won't bring immediate cashflow into your business; that is okay. It may take some time. But, do ask yourself, "How long will it take to see a return?" We live in a nanosecond world. We want things right now. All business decisions do not create immediate results. If the open door can lead to new a audience, referrals, brand recognition, product exposure, partnerships … that will eventually generate cashflow.

Keep track of what all you are doing, so you know what produces results and why. Do split testing, change a word, or a picture, or a color scheme, and test again to see the difference in results. Many marketing studies showed changing one word made a difference of several thousand dollars in an ad campaign for a product.

4) When I open this door, whom will be on the other side?

Flexibility and strength go hand-in-hand. In business, just as in life, it is key to have the right people surrounding you. If you are a strong person, look to balance your strength with someone who might be a bit more flexible. This will allow you to see things in a different light, maybe bend and balance when needed to, and find compassion. If you are too flexible, look for someone with a keen strength to help hold you to your goals. You will build self-confidence and your business/brand all at the same time!

I co-own a non-profit called Gratitude Girls (www.GratitudeGirls.com). We do a show the fourth Tuesday of every month. This is our opportunity to feature a special guest where we can we talk and, of course, share gratitude. I am very scheduled, organized, I like things "just so." I love especially being on the air, with a script and details of exactly what we are going to talk about when and why, etc.

My partner, Kathryn, loves to be spontaneous! She loves to talk off the cuff, from the heart, and always includes a part in our discussion this way. We both work together great because she appeases me by helping me as we go over what we are going to talk about and discuss, so we have a platform and a plan. And, at the same time, I am flexible. By being flexible, I appease her thus allowing the open discussion. It always works out wonderfully on our show, and I believe our guests and viewers love our hearts, compassion, and vulnerability we show by knowing each other.

We create a unity by sharing our needs and meeting the needs of each other. This is a partnership. And, every business opportunity stems from and creates a partnership. When you are relationship minded, business flows more easily. Now, business is not just about making others happy. Remember happiness is a choice. Instead, as business owners, employers, entrepreneurs, we strive to provide opportunities for our customers to find something they need, use it effectively, and create a relationship in the process.

Why is this relationship key? When we have a bond with another person, something amazing happens. We feel that connection. That connection keeps customers coming back even when they are getting "better deal emails" or "sold" at a networking event.

We buy from those we like and trust. Trust isn't created in an instant. True and real trust takes time and effort. When you put effort into your business relationships and customer service, your customers/clients take notice. They see your dedication. They hear your words matching your actions. And, they feel trust toward you. On another note, they like you. Can you hear Sally Field's Oscar acceptance speech, "You like me. You really like me!"

When you are in business you will develop haters, but it is important that you realize that you don't have to handle your detractors yourself. God will bless you right in front of them. All you can do with your haters is pray for them.

If you were stranded on a desert island and if you could pick one person to be sent to you, what kind of person would you wish to join you? The type of person you wish to join you tells you much about who you are at a core level, even in business. We tend to wish for people to be in our life who can bring strength where we are not strong, to bring patience when we are haste, to bring compassion when we need a shoulder, and most of all to envision our lives, our businesses, our relationships with us.

When we are real and honest and truly take a look at those we need in our lives, we see how we need to be to attract them, where we can be stronger, how we can give back, how we can be compassionate, and how we can grow as human beings, as mothers/fathers, as teachers, as friends, as leaders, as inspirational givers, and as business owners.

Chapter Number 6
Talking
We have the choice to do think before we speak

"Set a watch, O Lord, before my mouth; keep the door of my lips."

Psalm 141:3

Words are truly a reflection of our heart and our mindset. They show the respect we have for others as well as for ourselves.

Just as we can control — have the choice — what we put into our mouths, we must recognize, realize, and take ownership of what comes out of our mouths. We know the expression, "You are what you eat." Now, think about this, "Your heart is what you say."

What are your words saying about you? Are you thinking before you speak? Yes, sometimes we say things we regret, unfortunately, especially when we do not think before we open our mouths. But, we cannot take back the words said, someone cannot un-hear them. You can say you are sorry all you want, but that does not remove the fact that you said it, and did it deep down, just show what was truly on your heart?

> *"Every prudent man dealt with knowledge: but a fool layeth open his folly. A wicked messenger falleth into mischief: but a faithful ambassador is health"*
> **Proverbs 13:16 -17**

When we take the time to be wise with our words, we can create inspiration and joy. When we are quick to speak, we speak in harsh tones and lies that can hurt others. We are meant to live together on this Earth. We are meant to sharpen each other, to work together, and to lead others to joy and love.

There should never be excuses. "I said this because they said that." "I was really angry." "They hurt me first." "I was just being honest with my feelings." Oh, how the excuses can go on and on!

Many times in life, we talk, text or even post to social media, things before we think about them, and the possible consequences of our words to others. I remember when I was little my Mom would always tell me, "Think before I speak." Such wise words. Words we need to and must take more seriously. God tells us to control our tongue.

When I was in church and in Sunday School, I would be taught the same thing, as well as never to say anything or write anything that would not be pleasing to God.

As I got older and studied personal development and training, I would also learn and study things like if it does not lift someone up, help someone, etc, don't say it. If it is not true, do not say it; if it is not kind, do not say it.

Even if it is true, if it is not kind, then do not say it. Your tongue may be small in relation to your body, but is possesses the greatest strength.

"I beseech you therefore, brethren, by the mercies of God, that ye present your bodies a living sacrifice, holy, acceptable unto God, which is your reasonable service. And be not conformed to this world: but be ye transformed by the renewing of your mind, that ye may prove what is that good, and acceptable, and perfect will of God."

Romans 12:1-2

Although I am not perfect and I fall short of my Heavenly Father every day, I try my best to live by these principles. If am doing my best, I have the opportunity to be an example to others every singe day. The best I can.

The words that leave our mouths is a direct reflection of the state of our heart. If you are living with a "worldly heart," you are more likely to say worldly things. And, this world focuses on the "Me-Mentality!" We live in a world when people are doing and saying whatever they want to say despite the consequence, desire the effects it may have on those around us.

There is life and death in the power of our tongue. It is not necessarily what goes into a person that defiles him/her; it is what comes out of him/her. Think about that for a moment. I will say it again, the words we say are a direct reflection of our heart.

> *"Heaviness in the heart of man taketh it stoop: but a good word maketh it glad."*
> **Proverbs 12:25**

What makes your heart glad? Sometimes it is as simple as that — treating others as we want to be treated.

I remember someone said something to me very hurtful one day, it made me cry. They were sorry. They told me they were sorry and they didn't mean it. I wanted to believe them. I did forgive them, but at the same time, I still wondered, is that truly how they feel in their heart?

Our words are stones or blessings. If we choose to use them as stones, we simply become stone throwers with each word we speak. Some words can even be as swords! Swords are sharp and they cut! Do your words cut? Are they sharp? When we think before we speak, we can make better word choices. When we choose to speak blessings, we become brilliant gardeners helping others bloom!

Your words can literally impact someone's entire life. We must take time to ask ourselves a few questions before we speak (or write, post, share).

Am I being lazy when it comes to my words?

Words hold this power because we give words meaning. The issue happens when we give words different meaning then the person to whom we are speaking. Because we hold different meanings because of experiences we have generated over the course of our lives, we must be careful with our words.

As children (and I may be dating myself), we used to hear, "Sticks and Stones may break my bones, but words will never hurt me."

Why were we taught this? It is a defense mechanism when other are "mean" to us, when others say things intended to hurt our feelings or cause pain, when others are simply lazy with their words. But words can hurt! Granted if we allow them to. We must be careful what we say, but we must also be careful on how we react to others words said to us, and even our own words said to us!

In John 15, Jesus asked Peter, "Do you love me?" He asked Peter this three times. The first two times he used the same word for love. The third time he used a different word for love — a different meaning of love.

In the English language we just say "love." And, it is up to the two people communicating to see if their perceptions of the word are the same. We must look at tone of the voice and context of which the word is being said. Love can mean as a friend. Love as "in love." Love as a parent loves a child. Love like a child loves a parent/grandparent. Love as you like something very much. Love as our "things." Love as you love your "brother." Love as in we love God.

Jesus knew exactly what he meant to say. The first two times he asked Peter is what an "agape" love … a Godly love. The third it was different. Jesus asked Peter from a "phileo" love … brotherly love. Why the difference? Jesus wanted to be Peter's eternal brother not just his Savior/Messiah.

What exactly do I want and need to share?

We self-talk up to 500 words per minute. Not everything we think should be shared. Can you imagine talking to someone at the rate of 500 words per minute? I do believe we would all be walking around in overwhelm. Our eyes wide open. Our heads pounding from the knowledge and information shared. Our mouths dry.

This is not a pleasant feeling or picture. Could you handle hearing 500 words in one minute or even a few minutes?

As we think about the words we want to share, let's think about the meaning of those words and the why we are sharing. Are we sharing to inspire? Are we sharing to hurt? Are we sharing to self-promote? Are we sharing because our words could help someone? Does the person to whom I am speaking want and need to hear what I am about to say?

Have you ever been speaking with someone and one of two things happen? You say, "I don't know why I shared that?" Or they say, "I don't know what led me to share that with you? I have never told anyone that!"

Yes. In those moments, the person sharing wasn't thinking. The words weren't being thought about, they were simply being spoken. Once words are out there, we cannot suck them back in with a vacuum cleaner. (Even though many of us wish we could.)

Take a few seconds to think when you are in a conversation. When you are enjoying alone time, process upcoming conversations and business engagements to be prepared.

Now, what words have I been using and what words should I be using?

If we were to record our words over the course of several days, what would we find about how we speak, the words we use, and the tonality we speak?

Words come with every part of our life. Whether you are joking with friends or you seek to be completely honest (no sugar coating the situation), you still have to be cautious of the way in which you say things.

The next thing we know we are speaking doubt instead of faith. We've substituted the faith that was in our heart and replaced it with doubt. This second confession will nullify the first confession of faith, and render it void. It doesn't have to be this way. Hold fast to what you believe.

What words will I use?

In your words, be consistent in what you say. You words can tear someone down into pieces or you can chose to have them build someone up. When our words contain beauty people treasure them.

When you are deciding what words to use, think about this: What mood am I in currently? If we make decision or say things out of haste, anger, disappointment, jealousy, or just in a negative mood, we will more than likely regret the words used.

Now, what we choose to put into our minds through our eyes and ears will eventually come out. To understand what words we will use out of reaction, we must look at the words, attitude, the types of music, movies, television shows, books, and friends we are bringing into our lives.

We are called to guard our minds and our hearts. If you are around negative people, guess what? Yes, you will be negative. You want to be around them less. You feel drained many times or wore out after being around them.

When you choose to be with positive, happy, and productive people, you will take on those characteristics as well. You will also feel just overall better. You will many times want to be around those people more and more.

This is why they say, "You are the sum total of the 5 people with whom you spend your time." Want to know more about you, take a look at those 5 people!

These questions and this chapter must also be used on yourself. We doubt ourselves more than anyone (in most situations). We have hurt so many times we want others to hurt with us. We lose faith and want company in that. We know we are speaking doubt instead of speaking in faith. Doubt replaced faith in our hearts. When we have the courage to face this and admit it, amazing things will happen in our lives: in our minds, hearts, desires, and actions. It is time to hold true to your faith and what you believe.

What about when you are speaking to yourself? Do these hold true then? Yes. It is important that we master the relationship with ourselves before we try to do it with anyone else. Learning to speak kind thoughts to you may be one of the hardest and most rewarding things you will ever do. Learning to speak kind begins when you leave complaints behind.

If you were to write down each and every feeling you believe you experience in one week, how many feelings would it be? In this exercise, some people write down only five feelings/emotions, while others fill up a paper in a 60-second time limit. The test comes when you look at the feelings and emotions before you and you count the emotions/feelings that are negative and count the ones that are positive. What would your ratio being. As Americans, as human beings, as people … the ratio falls higher toward the negative feelings.

This is what you expect to feel over the course of a week? That is where people get stuck. They have these negative feelings and emotions because they are stuck in a place of hurt instead of moving toward a place of peace and healing. We let our hurt work for us instead of choosing to work for ourselves … to be our own "greatest cheerleader." To heal, it does take effort. To heal we do have to be stern, yet loving with our hearts and our minds. We need to find someone we can trust to speak freely with. Just to get things off our chest … think about that statement. Off our chest. What organ "lives" in your chest? Your heart, right! We must choose to release the pain from our hearts to heal. This might look like sharing words and thoughts that get you out of your comfort zone.

We know we are getting out of our comfort zone when our throat hurts. That is our mind and our heart trying to choke down the words we need to say, the words we must face. You can't face them until you get them "off of your chest." Once your have gotten these feelings, emotions, thoughts, etc off of your chest, the need for negativity leave the building! Yes, Elvis has left the building! :)

So, let me share with you again, *"Learning to speak kind begins when you leave complaints behind."* Complaints cause unneeded pain in your heart, your mind, and when you share them with others, they cause unneeded with them as well. No one desires to hangout or talk with someone who complains all the time. Many times we can be our worst self-critic. Do you know someone who fits this description?

Instead of just calling them out ... let's watch our words with them. Be the example. Show them what they have by complimenting them! In every person you come across, see what you can find, on how to compliment them on one thing, anything, but make sure it is a true and genuine compliment. People will feel loved, and when people around you feel loved you feel more loved.

You have a choice in how you act, react, and interact with them. Remember from Chapter 1, 87 percent of what we see and hear is negative. Let's change that together. We start by being the 13 percent someone needs in their lives. Maybe we need in our own life!

If they don't get the hint or seem to be closed off to making different choices for their lives, maybe, in love, it would be time to have a deeper conversation with them. And, keep being the 13 percent they need!

When someone says something positive to you, linger on those words on that thought for a few moments. How do you feel? How do you see yourself in those words? Try them on for a few moments like you are trying on a new pair of shoes.

You feel pretty amazing, right! Now keep this in mind when you speak to others. Be the new pair of awesome shoes for someone else! Life is about practicing gratitude. When you are talking, chose to express your gratitude for others, your relationships, for the opportunity to share and grow together.

Choose your words with wisdom. Choose them with happiness. Choose your words with compassion. Choose them with joy. Choose your words with health. Choose them with movement of the heart and silence of the mind. You have the choice.

Chapter Number 7
Relationships - Personal
We have the choice to build our personal relationships

We make choices every single day in our life, on how we treat our loved ones, and those in our lives closest to us. Are you choosing to enhance your personal relationships or hurt them?

Many times, as they say, we hurt those closest to us. It doesn't have to be that way, and it shouldn't be that way. The ones who God gave to us, especially, should be treated with our highest and best!

> *"With all lowliness and meekness, with longsuffering, forebearing one another in love, endeavouring to keep the unity of the Spirit in the bond of peace."*
> **Ephesians 4:2-3**

Our spouse or significant other (from here on I will just say spouse rather than being repetitive, knowing it can mean partner, etc), should also be our best and closest friend in the world. God created man and then created woman to be "an help meet for him". A woman should complete a man. As the saying goes, behind every good man, is a great woman. It is true! Man can be good; woman can be good. Together they can be great! (Now granted they can be great alone, too). But if you have someone in your life, they should lift you higher and push you to be more successful than you already are, and to your best, and vice-versa.

When you talk about your spouse with other people, do you life them up? Or, do you tear them down? It is a choice! None of us ever have a perfect relationship, but there are limits to who we should ever share any negative information to. Most times, anything positive can be and should be shared with everyone, while negative should only be shared with God in prayer.

Granted there are some situations where even negative things (like abuse, whether physical, spiritual, mental, or emotional) needs to be shared (must be shared) with a proper authority, pastor, police officer, counselor. I am not ever saying anything against this. Please know that if you are in a situation such as this, you must get help. Please get help. I implore you to take this action … choose to take this action for yourself.

How you choose to speak about your spouse to others reflects on your heart as well as your actions. It also pre-frames those listening to how they should perceive your spouse. They will look at your spouse differently. They could choose to walk away from a friendship, a friendship God intended to be a good and positive friendship.

The Bible is clear about leading others astray. Instead, guide others to see the positive in your spouse. You saw something positive. That is why you married them or are with them.

We have choices how to look for our spouse. We conveniently forget about the meaning of the word "pursue" along with how that looks in our lives. We pursue our dreams, our goals, our desires. Yet, we forget about pursuing our spouse.

Women, you know when we were dating, we'd get all dressed up for him, wear our best clothes, makeup, hair done, etc. Then, after marriage and babies, many times, we meet him at the door in a sweats. Or worse, let him come find us when he gets home!

Granted as wives and moms, we get busy! Taking care of kids, the house, and for some like me, our businesses we ran from home too! We also need to remember, he is usually out in the world working, and in front of lots of women who get dressed up and made up to go to work.

Many times these women don't mind if a man is married and some even prefer married men.

How did you pursue your spouse? It was that pursuit that attracted him to you! We want to make the choice to be the first to greet him at the door! Make the choice to look great, keeping him the way we got him. When we show him we care about the way we look, asking him what he likes, he feels important. Maybe he likes make up. Maybe he prefers you naturally. Knowing him means you have to talk to him. Good communication is key! Men must feel important! It is that idea, that we believe in him that keeps his heart longing for us and not looking outside for what he has at home.

Single girls, I say the same to you. When I was a little girl, my daddy cared how his girls were dressed and looked. So as we get older, not only for ourself too, but also our Heavenly Father. We are showing respect to Him when we look nice and care about our looks. Remember our body is a temple. And, in essence, our body belongs to our spouse.

I remember when I was married, many times, working from home, and taking care of kids, I still got up each morning. Being one to never stay in my pajamas (no matter how pink and cute), I would get dressed for the day, right away. Now granted, if I was staying home all day, I might not get all that dressed up, but right before my husband would come home from work, many times I would change clothes, fix my hair, and do my makeup. Why? Because my man was coming home, and I wanted to look pleasing to him. Many women get dressed up to go out, which granted, I do too, I like to always look nice. But if we do like to look nice when we go out, where other men (and women) will see us, why don't we for when we are at home, where our, hopefully, the most important man in our life will see us?

Same goes for men, keep her how you got her. Women must be pursued. You can pursue them through act of love. Women must see and hear your love and affection. Before marriage, you took her our on dates, treated her like a princess, told her how beautiful she is, gave her winks, and made her stomach flutter with butterflies. You didn't just show her affection to "get affection." You wrapped her with love and affection because you saw how she sparkled and shined when you did. You did it for her … not for you.

> *"Thou hast my heart, my sister, my spouse; you have ravished my heart with one of thine eyes, with one chain of thy neck."*
> **Song of Solomon 4:9**

There are many types of affection. Keep the affection PG to show her true love and respect. And, when you take the time to ask her how her day was, what she wants ... and you listen ... not doubting or trying to change her mind ... watch and experience what happens next.

Those things should not stop because you put a ring on "it" and a paper from government. You shouldn't stop pursuing and dating just because finances are tight. There are always lots of free things to do! Never stop because you've been married awhile (longer than you can remember :)). Keep her the way you got her. You will thank me later!

> *"Two are better than one, because they have a good reward for their labor: For if they fall, the one will lift up his fellow: but woe to him that is alone when he falleth; for he hath not another to help him up. Again, if two lie together, then they have heat: but how can one be warm alone?"*
> **Ecclesiastes 4:9-11**

When I was married, my husband and I had dates every single week. When the kids were tiny and I was nursing, the youngest one many times went with us. Yet, we still went! Did you read that? We still went! We were lucky to have my mom and mother-in-law both live close, so the kids could visit grandma and grandpa every once in a while so we could go out on a date. And, of course, there were times when finances were tight. During these tough times, we would just go for a drive, go to the park, or go for a walk together, hand-in-hand. "PG affection"

Now, building your personal relationships is not just about building the relationship between you and your spouse. Building personal relationships can simply mean friends!

How do you treat your friends? Do you take the time to check in or do you allow life to consume and get in the way? What words do you use when you are speaking to your friends? How about when you are speaking about your friends?

> *"Charity suffereth long, and is kind; charity envieth not; charity vaunteth not itself, it is not puffed up, doth not behave itself unseemly, seekers not her own, is not easily provoked, thinkers no evil"*
> **1 Corinthians 13:4-5**

We never know exactly what someone is going through. We only know what they care to share with us.

When I was in high school, I was a cheerleader. Many people cheer for their favorite teams. We should be a cheerleader for our spouse, for our children, and our friends. We have the choice to uplift them with empowering words that will help and push them to greater and greater success and new heights.

And, we have the power to tear them down, especially family, we are closest to them, we live with them, we see each others flaws the most. We know how to hurt them. We know how to hurt them because something we once "idolized" in them is now something we "demonize." Yes, we like all those cute faults in the beginning because we are thinking about the future. We aren't thinking about those future needs being met. We are thinking in the now.

We can sometimes get lazy in our relationships. Lazy creates excuses, yet love makes a way.

It is our choice to how we treat those special people in our lives ... how we treat the strangers too!

It is a simple word ... R.E.S.P.E.C.T.! Are you singing it with me?

When you show respect to others, you are really saying to the world, "I respect myself." Choose to treat others with politeness and kindness. Encourage them when they need it. Always listen to others before taking time to "interrupt" or share your own view point. No one likes an interruptor! Once you have taken the time to listen, show that. Tell the person with whom you are speaking how their idea inspire, how they can use their ideas to change the world!

I know we have all heard this, "Treat others as you would want to be treated." This is a very hard task in the world/society in which we live. I see people running red lights. I watch cars not pull over for police officers, fire trucks, and ambulances. These non-stoppers would be the first to complain if someone didn't pull over if they were in the back of the ambulance or if the fire truck was on the way to pull them out of a car accident using the jaws of life.

As you watch these selfish actions, how do you practice compassion and understanding and love for them? They are obviously not treating others with respect or the way they would want to be treated.

The Bible is clear about praying for enemies. It is easy to pray for those we love, those for whom we care. We see a benefit in that. Praying for someone who just did you wrong … well … that is another story. I believe I just took a big deep breath as I typed that.

It is another story. A story of grace because we have been given grace. A story of power because we have the power in how we choose to treat others. A story of compassion because we need compassion everyday. A story of strength because we must use our love, compassion, use your "grace" muscle every day to keep it working properly. It is another story because when extend prayer for those who wronged us, we are seeing glimpses of heaven, of Jesus, and God in our own life.

We are seeing what making positive choices in our life can do! Whatever you are searching for, no matter what it is, you will find it or create it. We must remain focused on the positive, on the steps that bring us closer together and further along in the journey. Protecting our personal relationships is key to creating and maintaining in our lives.

Enemies are everywhere. Yes, the battlefield is everywhere. Instead of getting comfortable, choose to get and remain bold.

"Let love be without dissimulation. abhor that which is evil; cleave to that which is good. Be kindly affectioned one to another with brotherly love; in honor preferring one another; not slothful in business; fervent in spirit; serving the Lord."
Romans 12:9-11

Even on those days we feel absolutely lost, keeping a positive attitude will bring us back to the path with a renewed strength, an unforeseen wisdom, and heart ready to give compassion and grace. When you are called to move, you will be ready!

Chapter Number 8
Relationships - Business
We have the choice to build our business relationships

Are you underrating yourself? When it comes to building relationships in business, you must build confidence in your abilities. Be clear about the positiveness you bring to the table, to the relationship.

Scarcity comes in many form, and it affects all areas of our life and business.

When you give your best, the rest will be blessed. We must be prepared for relationships. Being prepared greatly increases the chance for success. And, in business, we need and desire successful relationships.

> *"No man hath seen God at any time. If we love one another, God dwellers in us, and His love is perfected in us."*
> **1 John 4:12**

According to investopedia.com, the definition of a business relationship reads like this, "refers to the connections formed between various stakeholders in the business environment, including relations between employers and employees, employers and business partners, and all the companies with which a company is associated".

Building relationships means gardening to grow meaningful connections. Instead of just hanging out, dilly-dallying at networking opportunities, know you have to make friends and meet acquaintances.

Notice I did not say go to networking events to meet people to try to sell them your product or service. If you are not networking to build relationships, you are merely socializing.

I love the idea of the connection formed. How cool is that! A connection is formed from honesty, realness, authenticity and communication. A successful connection is formed when you show you genuinely care. How do you show you care?

1. Take notice! How can you take notice? Identify Like-Minded Goals and Values. When you are connecting or meeting someone, take the time to say to yourself, "I am in this place at this specific moment, why? Why am I here and What can I do with it?"

"A good man sheweth favour, and lendeth: he will guide his affairs with direction."
Psalm 112:5

2. Get Social and mean it! On social media ... friend like you mean it ... and don't forget about the rest of the list. Don't just be the one-night charmer. When we meet people who are overly charming, our guard can go up. Yes, charmed I'm sure! Social media is about being connected. Truly connected. Do you post just to see how many likes and comments you will get? Or do you post to genuinely share your heart and values with other in an effort to help and educate or lift someone else up? Same thing with liking and commenting on others posts. Are you doing it to genuinely build that relationship with them? People are smart, they can see right through if you are being genuine or not.

"Thou shalt not defraud they neighbor, neither rob him: the wages of him that is hired shall not abide with thee all night until the morning."
Leviticus 19:13

3. Live in your solar system with a galaxy-minded spirit. You be the connector. Schedule time together: to have fun and to brain storm. As a business owner, entrepreneur, marketing professional, sales coordinator — you are meant to shine. Building your house on a hill allowing yourself to be seen! You can share and show love, your greatness and what all God as done for you, without being prideful (make sure to be careful of that, as God gives, he can take away as well). I have been very blessed in my web, graphics and marketing

business....anytime I mention anything about it, I mention, I prayed and asked God to teach me and help me, back in 1993, and i would use it for Him. He answered, and I always mention my blessings and how I learned so well, is due to God allowing it. I am very thankful and grateful, and try to always give the Glory to Him, and in that try to share and show others, when we trust in Him, and do the work too (He doesn't say just pray and wait) then He is righteous and will bless. God says we should show and share our blessings and show what God has done for us, we can be a great example to others of faith. He says to show your light, not to hide it. God wants to use you, to show His light to others. Don't hide your blessings, don't be prideful and count them as yours either.....Show and share them, and show God's goodness, and give the credit where the credit is due. Anything you have, has come from the blessings God allowed you to have.

"Ye are the light of the world. A city that is set on a hill cannot be hid. Neither do men light a candle, and put it under a bushel, but on a candlestick; and it giveth light unto all that are in the house. Let your light shine before men, that they may see your good works, and glorify your Father which is in Heaven."

Matthew 5:14-16

4. Follow the Path ... Follow Up and Follow Through. Offer to be, to do, offer something before you ask for

anything! When we take time to educate others, give them bits of wisdom from our experience/knowledge/expertise, when we take the time to inspire others, when we take the time to help others in ways we know we can, we are building the foundation for trust. Trust is what creates a relationships that endure.

Think about God ... his love endures forever.

5. It is okay to let go. We must covet what we have and not what we have lost.

Relationships determine much about your life. They lead the path to job offers you will receive. They present themselves in the consulting/business contracts and clients you attract. They even determine the business opportunities knocking at your door. Where we falter is we forget about strategy. Business Relationships can be "chess like!" (if you like games) Or, even like cultivating a garden (if you like gardening). When we are gardening, we have to pull weeds. Pulling weeds is essential to allowing the other plants to flourish!

"Let all bitterness, and wrath, and anger, and clamour, and evil speaking, be put away from you, with all malice; and be ye kind one to another, tenderhearted, forgiving one another, even as God for Christ's sake hath forgiven you"
Ephesians 4:31-32

The quality of your business relationships is based on the energy and focus you choose to put into them. You now have 5 ways to start focusing that energy today. You can make your business relationships more beneficial and more productive!

Chapter Number 9
Thinking
We have the choice to think positively or negatively, prosperously or poorly

Make a choice to be more mindful. You are, in fact, what you think. We create what we think. Is this scary to you? Or, are you feeling blessed? It is okay if it is scary to you. It takes time, effort, and practice to take control of our thoughts. The thing is, every thought, you have the choice, to pay attention, and allow it to take you one way, or another, positive or negative, and you can make that new choice, with every single thought. Once you are and become more aware of this, it is easier to consciously make the right choice to choose to lean toward the positive side.

> *"And all things, whatsoever ye shall ask in prayer, believing, ye shall receive"*
> **Matthew 21:22**

Some may want to teach you how to "rule" your mind. Because, we aren't technically designed to rule over ourselves. I, instead, believe that we must choose to control our mind, our thoughts, and thus our actions. God actually commands this of us as well....He tells us to think of things of that are good, we posted this before, but it is a good reminder.

> *"Finally, brethren, whatsoever things are true, whatsoever things are honest, whatsoever things are just, whatsoever things are pure, whatsoever things are lovely, whatsoever things are of good report; if there be any virtue, and if there be any praise, think on these things."*
> **Philippians 4:8**

How do we get to place when we feel comfortable controlling our thoughts. How do we practice this?

1. When you feel the urge to let your thoughts control you, take a few minutes to simply sit and be. Do your best to empty your mind as you are letting go of the negative thoughts. Meditation is many times thought to be a happiness booster of sorts. Once you are sitting and have silenced your mind, focus on shifting your brain activity from the right frontal area, which has been associated with depression, worry, anxiety; to the left, which has been found to be associated with happiness, excitement, and joy. Make yourself smile. Try it, look in the mirror and smile at yourself. It is very hard to keep a bad thought or feeling when you are smiling.

"Where there is no vision, the people perish: but he that keepeth the law, happy is he."
Proverbs 29:18

When my mother was diagnosed with Stage 4 cancer, I went searching — reading and researching for her — looking for all natural things to help and heal her. I found so many things on the mind — your thoughts.

It is funny how life comes full circle. My mom is the one who taught me many of these things when I was younger. I can hear her voice now, "Be careful what you think about - it may come about." The kids' church songs "Be careful little eyes what you see; be careful little ears what you hear."

2. When you feel your thoughts controlling you, know it is okay to stay in that moment until you take control back. Change your thoughts. Put that negative thought in a bubble and blow it away. Replace it with a positive thought that will create success in your life.

3. As you practice controlling your thoughts, put yourself in a familiar, happy, joyful, positive environment/situation.

4. Write down what triggers negative emotions or outburst.

5. Take control of your thoughts by guarding them. Sometimes knowledge is truly wasted on the young they say, I say giving knowledge to others, no matter the age, if it is truth, you are helping them and you never know many times who you are helping without even knowing it. As I got older, I started to study and read more, I read many times about guarding your mind.

The first book my mom ever got me as an adult was, *You Cannot Afford the Luxury of a Negative Thought.*

Experts say that 87 percent of what we hear and see is negative, so we need to protect ourselves and shield ourselves. My kids had the whole outfit — the entire armor of God. Yes, Bryan and I taught and preached this to our kids, and I continue with this today with my children (even as they become adults).

> *"For God hath not given us the spirit of fear; but of poor, and of love, and of a sound mind."*
> **2 Timothy 1:7**

How many of us keep teaching and preaching it to ourself? We are not exempt! If we have no vision, we will perish. This is for ALL of US, not just for churches. It is for each individual. What are your goals and visions for your life? Do you write them down? Journal about them?

If you don't write them down, they are simply dreams you wish to accomplish. Once you write them down, they become goals you set out to accomplish. Two different thoughts. One is wishing upon a star like Pinocchio or feeling that a dream is your heart's wish like Cinderella.

I highly recommend getting a journal, keeping it by your bedside, and every night before bed, write five specific things from that day for which you are grateful and thankful. Once we are thankful, we can learn and grow. Once you have completed the five thankfuls, write five specific things on which you are working, "as if ye have already received" in the present tense, believing that you already have them as the Bible teaches, and then just journal for another five minutes, on whatever comes to your mind.

We have the choice to think prosperously. What we say to ourself in our own minds, can be so detrimental, or it can be so powerful and helpful. When you are paying your bills, are you in a grateful state of mind, being thankful and grateful, for example, the electricity and the power to be able to cook your food, see at night, etc (our families before us didn't have that!) or do you say to yourself that you can't believe how high that bill is?

Do you say, "Everything and everybody prospers me now, and I prosper everything and everybody now."? That is an abundance mindset, you are not only saying for yourself, but you are also saying for everyone else around you.

Choosing how we think does take time and training. Just as train our bodies to run marathons/5k's/weight light, we must train our minds. Training equals commitment. Training is a decision to work on it every day, every chance we get.

Make the commitment now. As the sun rises … as the light goes down … as the stars shine … as the moon hides, you have control over your thoughts and your mind. When you find your mind go the wrong way, don't beat yourself up, just re-focus and think right, it is always as simple as that, controlling and adjusting your mind, and making a conscious choice to think the way that is best for you.

No matter what people say to you or say about you. Use it. Practice it. And, it is okay if you have a day that isn't perfect. We all have them. We all try our best. When you truly do your best … your best is good enough. You are good enough. You are worth so much more than you see.

When you focus on what others say, that is when you will stumble! A friend shared with me a story recently, and I thought about what I was writing and sharing with you in this chapter.

She played high school basketball. During her first high school varsity game, she learned an extremely valuable lesson. She grabbed a rebound. Put the ball to the floor and sprinted down the court. She was in the middle of a fast break. No one near her. Instead of focusing on the back board, the basket, and the ball, she turned her head. She turned her head back. She had another player gaining on her. She stumbled by looking back. The fast break was lost.

The Apostle Paul says we're like runners in a race and only one receives a prize at the event, we must run as if we deeply desire to "obtain it." To obtain it we must never look backwards. When we focus on what is in front of us, we choose to leave the past behind us. Just like in a car, we should use the rear-view mirror to glance at, maybe review a life lesson, to not do again, but not focus there - we are to focus forward, through that big picture window, and move forward. God talks about this as well, talking about Lot's wife, when she turned and looked back, she was made into salt. We are to always be moving forward.

> "But his wife looked back from behind him, and she became a pillar of salt"
> **Genesis 19:26**

It may be time to leave those negative thoughts behind. Now granted, notice, I did not say "move on," on purpose. I have had others make comments to me about "moving on." With anything in life, but especially in the steps of a widow, to me, my opinion, moving on, is like as if we divorced and I am getting on with my life.

Well, we did not divorce, but we can no longer obviously be together, and I do think it is very important to move "forward". Your thoughts reflect your feelings, emotions, ideas of yourself. Have you have taken time to write down everything you think about you? Take time right now.

Write down your idea of who you are and who you are meant to be. I challenge you or even dare you (if that gets you to take action).

Once you have written down your ideas, thoughts, and feelings of who you are, circle the positive ones. ALL OF THEM. Rewrite them on a sheet a paper. Remember you are focusing on the positive ideas and feelings.

Crumble up the "older" paper. Throw away those negative thoughts and ideas. You are made new. You have chose to take this opportunity to create a positive you!

And, being made new is the most wonderful feeling in the world. It proves to your brain that you are worth it. Your brain, body, feelings, emotions, and ideas will believe what you tell it.

Someone else believes you are worth it as well ... keep reading. You are worth it!

Chapter Number 10

Jesus

We have the choice to follow, accept Jesus

Life is full of choices. This includes our decision on the afterlife. There is only one way to get to Heaven, the Bible talks about the straight and narrow path.

We are all sinners. We were born that way. Some of us sin worse than others, in our human eyes, but in God's eyes, sin is sin. Even the little white lies, is still sin. We first must realize that God says even the thought of sin, is sin. So even if we don't act on it, which of course is best, but the thought of it, is still sin. Have you ever thought of stealing something? Even a small pack of gum when you were a child? That was sin.

"For all have sinned, and come short of the glory of God."

Romans 3:23

There is a price for sin. God says there is a price. We must pay the consequences for anything we do in our lives. When my kids were young, we taught them there is always a consequence for anything you do, good or bad, of course the good consequences are the ones we always want and look forward to.

"For the wages of sin is death; but the gift of God is eternal life through Jesus Christ our Lord."

Romans 6:23

God always has something in store for you. That never fades. It is never in the past. He has something better than that relationship you fled. Has something better than food you shove in your mouth. He has something more amazing than those drugs/alcohol make you feel. What He has for you is bigger than your fears and your tears.

His plan for you and his gifts for you are more than your past mistakes.

Trust in Him. Trust Him.

*"Getting over a painful experience is much like crossing monkey bars.
You have to let go at some point in order to move forward."*
– C.S. Lewis.

Jesus died and rose again to pay for our sins. Jesus sacrificed Himself on the cross for us. Jesus is the only perfect man that never sinned, that ever walked the Earth. He is the only one pure enough to get us to Heaven. He lived his life on this earth, for us, for a purpose, to shed His blood, so we could go to Heaven when we die, if we choose. But God still gives us that free will to choose. He wants to be chosen, just like we want others to choose to like us, love us, be with us, and share life together. God wants the same. You were after all created in His image. Think about that for a moment. God wants to be chosen ... just like you do. He has already chosen you. Now you must take the next step.

"But God commendeth His love toward us in that while we were yet sinners, Christ died for us."

Romans 5:8

God will save you if you put your trust in Him. We are His children, He created us, He wants us to live with Him, but He gave us that free will of choice. Kind of like our kids, we (hopefully, i know I do) love my kids, and want them close to me always; I am very family oriented. Once they grow up and become adults, they have the choice of how close to us they want to be. We still will always love them from afar, if that is the path they choose. So will God with us. But he wants that personal relationship with us.

"For whosoever shall call upon the name of the Lord shall be saved."

Romans 10:13

It says whosoever, that means anyone and you are "anyone." It doesn't matter what you've done or where you've been. If (and when) you call upon the name of the Lord, He is right there for you.

Now of course, this doesn't mean go out and do whatever you want, just because. God still says there are consequences for all sin, and you will pay for your actions. He wants us to do right, but no matter what, He will be there for us. Just like many times, we want our kids to do right, in the end, usually, no matter what, we will still love our kids and be there for them.

If you have not ever trust God and asked Him to come into your heart. I would challenge you to do so. It is so simple, just say something like, "Dear Jesus, I know that I am a sinner, and because of that sin, I deserve Hell. But Jesus, please save me, and take me to Heaven with you one day when I die. Jesus, I am trusting you, and only You to take me to Heaven. Amen."

Jesus freely gave. He made His choice to give His life for you. Unconditional. You had to do absolutely nothing. The only "religion" you can't earn. We can't earn love, but we can make choices to keep the relationship ... with ourselves, with others, with our bodies, our food, and of course, for our eternity.

Choosing You
Today is not an end; it is a beginning. Start today!

Life is full of choices. We have the opportunity to make choices each and every second of the day. You made the choice to pick up this book. You then made the choice to read it. Read it all the way through! If I was there with you, I could give you a high-five because you took ownership of your decision and saw it all the way to the end. To the conclusion, in fact! :)

What I hope you gained from your choice is that your journey doesn't have to come from you. Instead, you have the choice to allow your journey to come through you. It is a choice. And, this choice makes a difference.

When you allow your journey to come through you, you are allowing God to work in an amazing ways, to bring good, to turn pain into beauty, a beauty we can all see. I look at the "pains" in my life, those losses, the hurts, and the negative choices I made. Then, I look at how my life shifted, by a choice. A choice I chose to make, one step at a time, on each different road I was on at the time.

A choice to become healthy in all areas of my life. A choice to allow God to work. My journey comes through me and now can carry through to you, to positively impact the choices of your life.

How do you envision deciding to have joy in your life? What choices will you make the next time you are faced with putting healthy or non-healthy food in your mouth? Hitting the snooze alarm or jumping out of bed with a bright attitude on life? Health is more than food and exercise, it is balance. How can you choose to work on achieving balance in all areas?

Now that you have written down your business goals and you have solid advice on taking new opportunities, where can your decision take your business? Everything we do in our lives involves words. What words are you speaking to yourself? To others? Are you speaking life? Speak life. Always speak life because our words set into motion the rest. When you speak life, balance happens. Business increases. Your health sparkles. Choosing to exercise is natural. You crave healthy food. And, before you know it, you are choosing JOY!

If you were upset by any of your circumstances before you read this book, you have a different, more positive view now. You know you hold the keys. You have an new found fierce joy. Keep that fierce joy because being "luke warm" for anything is the worst possible place to be. Luke warm is a sense of being complacent and stuck. None of us like a luke warm bath right? We want it hot! Nice and hot; cleansing and soothing.

Today is a new beginning. Each day you wake up to a new world. A new world brings with it a fresh start. You got this. Others' minds can inspire us — but only us — yes, you/me in the moment (this moment) can motivate us ... get us to take action. **Remember, today you are choosing You!** Find a victory in today. In fact, find a victory in each and every day. You are worth the fight ... the fight for victory!

Never let anyone shame you. Instead, choose to let others empower you. Own your decision. Own it because you are worth it. Own it because you were not created and designed to be ordinary. You were created and designed to be Extraordinary. You are worth it. I am worth it. We are here to make a difference in the world, for good. Let's find it, and share it, and choose to make the best of our dash while we are here.

Send me a message of what you got out of this book, connect with me, share your steps on your roads with me. www.LaurieDelk.me

I look forward to hearing how you smile, even though sometimes through tears, in your steps, on each road you take. Blessings!